POLITE ESSAYS

Date Due

DEC 2 1969		
DEC 1 2 1970		

EZRA POUND

POLITE ESSAYS

Essay Index Reprint Series

BOOKS FOR LIBRARIES PRESS, INC.

FREEPORT, NEW YORK

First published 1937
Reprinted 1966

CONTENTS

I

HAROLD MONRO[1]

'Alas, my broder, so mote it be.'

The evil done by Ste Beuve is considerable and incalculable. It has allowed every parasite and nitwit to present himself as a critic, and thousands of essayists incapable of understanding a man's work or his genius have found opportunity in a discussion of wash lists.

I doubt if any death in, or in the vicinity of, literary circles could have caused as much general regret as that of Mr Harold Monro, among people who had no exaggerated regard for his writing. An analysis of the why need not necessarily be taken as an excursion into criticism of pure letters. Monro was 'slightly known' as an author, widely known as a social worker in his particular line, and moderately, I suppose, known as an editor. One's strongest regret is for the passing of an honest man from a milieu where honesty, in the degree he possessed it, is by no means a matter of course.

In 1910 or 1911, or whenever it was that Mr Monro returned from Italy to evangelize his unappreciative nation, we used to distinguish him from most of his circle or from those authors whom he spasmodically admired, by saying that he alone among them suffered from his stupidity. The rest were unconscious and un-

[1] *The Criterion,* July 1932.

suspicious, but Harold by reason of his ten drops of Latin blood or his half-pint of Scots idem, was pervaded by a vague uneasiness in his sadness.

His gift for admiration was a danger, his earnestness was a danger, to himself that is. He would come to table one week with the portentous news that Wubbabua was a great author, two weeks later Bevidro was a great writer. These writers were inevitably dull with the dullness of all the Wordsworthian left over. Harold admired. We used also to say that Harold would get round to knowing it about five years after he had been told. I make that statement with no irony and no malice. His more-esteemed contemporaries have gone on for twenty years in unconsciousness and will die ultimately in their darkness. The world war startled a few of them into thought, the Russian revolution and the later fiscal calamities have perhaps clouded their declining years with a vague adumbration. The idea that words should define what they mention, that good letters have some significance in the health of the State, that poetry was before England, and so forth. All these were strange and damnable heresies. The milieu did not believe in ideas. The milieu believed in habit.

The sense that the country is ill because it can comprehend neither the revolution of the word nor the rectification of the word, is still alien to English sensibility.

In said milieu arrived Mr Monro with a confused belief that there ought to be literature or, perhaps one should say, national minstrelsy. The belief was probably in the phase: tradition. England a nest of singing birds. I doubt if any of us in 1911 clearly articulated the proposition: there ought to be an active literature for if its literature be not active, a nation will die at the top. When literature is not active; when the word is not constantly striving toward precision, the nation decays in its head. There may be to-day some conception of the nation as a whole, but the sense of the nation as a total intellectual organism is, to put it mildly, deficient. As for 'anyone'—especially anyone in the intermediate realm of print—feeling the slightest responsibility for the literary or intellectual health of England or of any other nation...even distinguished savants refer to the idea as 'an aurora borealis playing above the public'.[1]

Monro had at any rate some idea that there ought to be poetry in England, some hearth for it, moved possibly by memories of 'The Mermaid'. He had also another idea or moral predisposition which greatly complicated his life. He believed that 'these people' (in the particular recalled conversation 'people like Gosse') '*ought* to be —— useful'. An idea which might seem on the face of it sound, but which was far more difficult to bring into focus with the then or the now reality than the general lay-reader can be supposed to conjecture.

The methods of post-Victorian British literary politics were abruptly illuminated a couple of years ago by an exposition of documents and private letters in Paris, among them a missive from the late librarian of the House of Lords (Mr Gosse), asking the editor of *La Revue des Deux Mondes*, not to review or notice *Ulysses*.

Into this purgatory came Harold with a pure heart, a gloomy countenance and a passion for justice—with a slow, late-arriving smile and none of the consolations

[1] Private letter from Dr Breasted.

which stupidity accords to them who have it unwittingly.

During those early years I doubt if he ever received an idea clear at first go, or ever gripped it at once by the handle. He was of those exasperating editors who seem more or less to comprehend what they are told but who are two hours later told something else. His distinction being that he was, in this, perfectly honest and never faked acquiescence. I suppose he went wrong repeatedly. At any rate that was, I believe, current opinion, and his errors were by no means minimized by his habit of oracular utterance when and possibly whenever he had a conviction, in a voice pitched an octave or a tenth lower than is usual in mundane conversation. Not only that Wubbabua and Bevidro were great men, but in one soaring flight some years later that—was a journalist. He respected the critic but the verse wasn't poetry (almost with a German b, 'boedry'), it was journalism. Anything new gave him trouble.

Again, this is not a condemnation. He certainly did not die in his errors, or at least not in the errors that had been his in an earlier period. Every curate's egg that came to him, he ate to the uttermost to see whether there wasn't good in it somewhere. So that a few years ago he produced as expiation or monument, an anthology based on terrible knowledge, an anthology in which every worst and most damnable poet in England is shown with his best foot forward, some tatter of *pelle leonina* covering, at least some patch of ass-hide. Naturally a very unpopular book: all the second-raters and third- and fourth-raters furious to be relegated to their natural strata, and all the brighter lights disgruntled at being found in such company. A typical Monro product, a symbol of Harold's life, geographically, in Bloomsbury where he lived for a score of years and belonged to no gang.

We used to say that the tragedy of Harold was that he once wrote a good poem, but didn't like it and so destroyed it. That act was probably his distinction, it was a poem that conformed to some standard that wasn't his, or wasn't at that time his, and couldn't have been what he was driving at, and it was his method of keeping faith with himself.

One of the densest, almost ubiquitous, English stupidities of that time was the disbelief that poetry was an art. Dozens of blockheads expected the crystal Helicon to gush from their addled occiputs 'scientiæ immunes ...anseres naturali'.[1] Harold as usual took a middle course, he was willing to learn a little and very, very slowly. He never got any credit for his years of seniority. The English slowness in starting is a constant wonder to the foreigner. Whether it is from climate or from gentlemanly abhorrence of Sam Smiles, I know not; but you found, and find the young Englishman at twenty-eight or at thirty-two vaguely adumbrating, vaguely considering, whereas the more (I search for an adjective) I take no refuge in Pelman. Already Schiller's Don Carlos had given it tongue in 'Drei und zwanzig Jahre alt und nichts für Ewigkeit gethan!'

It was only in reading Harold's obituary notice that I discovered he was six years my elder, and that there was that much the more to his sorrow, he had chosen the worst time to live in, he had gone through the two

[1] *De Volg. Eloq.*

7

darkest *lustra*, or the three or more as you figure it: 1902 to 1908, 1920 to 1930.

He missed the fun of Hulme's dinners at the 'Tour Eiffel' 1909, and I do not remember him at Mrs Kibble-white's evenings in the old Venetian Embassy, then glass-factory house.

He took no part in the later endeavour to lackey-ize poetry and make it an adjunct to 'society'. I should say that he intrigued not at all. He sold nobody's books in his shop with enough vigour or partiality to make friends. On the other hand, he committed acts of independence, he suggested that justice be done to what I should call the better element among writers; in fact to those whom I then considered and still consider the only writers of poetry of the period who are worth ink or attention.

He did not make his shop an intellectual centre by reason of his stubbornness in refusing to sell anything but verse. He might have made it the foyer of several 'movements' or of several stirs. I don't think he ever really approved of them *while* they were active or exciting. Thus the active did him no honour.

On the other hand, the obstructors and obfuscators never pardoned him his tolerance of the active. He went so far as to import and publish sheets of *Des Imagistes*, the first anthology of that faith. Why he wasn't in it, I cannot at this time remember, unless it was that I had called him a blithering idiot or because he had clung to an adjective. Either at that time or later he certainly wrote poems that measured up to that standard, or at any rate without reconstructing the standard or re-examining the actual text, one remembers them as attaining the level desired. It may have been that I was strict, at that time, to the point of fanaticism. At any rate I committed only one error of inclusion (one poem, not his, that had been better omitted not, perhaps, so much for itself as for its subsequence).

After the 'Celtic Twilight', more or less definable or at least qualifiable, there came another sort of muddle or crepuscule; I should incline to say 'forgotten' or at least fairly forgettable. I doubt if anyone will get any credit for work done during that five years or that decade, or if there is much 'use' (in the general sense) in their having their accounts made up and presented for public estimation. Only in reading, in Harold's death notice, that he was this year fifty-three, does one consider that he belonged probably to the decade of Hewlett, Sturge Moore, Ernest Rhys and Fred Manning, a decade neither out nor in?

I don't know that there is much to be gained by writing or reading criticism of minor epochs, it may on the other hand be the best form of class-room exercise imaginable. You have a period of muddle, a few of the brightest lads have a vague idea that something is a bit wrong, and no one quite knows the answer. As a matter of fact Madox Ford knew the answer but no one believed him, certainly Mr Monro did not believe him. Mr Hulme is on the road to mythological glory; but the Hulme notes, printed after his death, had little or nothing to do with what went on in 1910, 1911 or 1912. Mr Yeats had set an example (specifically as to the inner form of the lyric or the short poem containing an image), this example is obscured for posterity and for the present 'young'—meaning Mr Eliot and his juniors—by Mr (early) Yeats's so very poetic language.

Mr Hueffer was getting himself despised and rejected by preaching the simple gallic doctrine of living language and *le mot juste*. His then despisers and neglectors are already more or less inexplicable to our (1932) contemporaries. I doubt if I could in any way convey their essence or accidents to the youth of the country (or to, at least, the youth of my country) on any other ground save that of their excessive, almost abnormal stupidity.

What is 'posterity' or the general reader or the reader in *any* foreign country ('aucun pays du monde'[1]) going to make of the following details?

1. Mr Prothero attempted to punish, and did indeed punish, me on my pocket for having demonstrated in favour of Lewis and Gaudier.[2]

2. I have heard Sturge Moore, certainly one of the most sensitive poetic susceptibilities of the period, contend that a man was as likely, perhaps more likely, to produce a good work of art on a bad theory than on a good one. He has printed a statement (*Quarterly Review*, if I remember correctly) that Flaubert had no sense of form. In conversation: that the shaping of the 'Trois Contes' into a whole, focused on the 'Lui vient l'idée d'employer son existence au service des autres' in St Julien, does not constitute form.

Consider also the following conversation with Hewlett as (*a*) evidence of state of mind among English *letterati* in the second decade of the century: (*b*) as evidence of 'Morrie's' personal charm, naïveté and humanity:

'*Hewlett* in praise of Newbolt likens N's works to "The Ballads".

[1] J. Cocteau.   [2] *Instigations*, p. 194.

E. P.: But . . . (blanks left for profanity) . . . it, Hewlett,
 look at the line:

   'He stood the door behind',

(blanks left for profanity) you don't find lines like that
 in Patrick Spence.

Hewlett: But, but I don't mean an Olde ballad, I mean
 an eh—eighteenth-century ballad.

E. P.: But (blanks left for profanity), Hewlett, the man
 is a contemporary of Remy de Gourmont!

Hewlett: Ungh!! Unh nnh, eh, I don't suppose he has
 thought of that. (Long pause)

Hewlett (continues very slowly): I don't suppose, eh,
 I had either.'

So it is one thing to estimate Monro's poetry, or anyone's poetry of that period, according to the high and
international and long durable standards, and quite
another to explain the uncertainties, *tâtonnements*, ad-
herences to locutions of late Victorian poesy, which are
to be found in nearly all work of those years. What was
a slow-witted, absolutely honest man to do in that
confusion? Measure his writing against even the best
work of a given month by the men with most definite
ideas, most conscious of going from somewhere to
somewhere else.

Let us say that Hewlett's 'Artemision' is junked, but
that those of us who remember him remember a poem
about Propertius and one about Gaubertz. Monro has
had some sort of acceptance.[1] 'Milk for the Cat' has, I
believe, appeared in 120 anthologies. The poem presents

---

[1] Some of his brief volumes of poems went into three editions,
and he was included in Benn's chamber of horrors.

a definite visual image, and, as far as I remember it, is a straight statement in perfectly simple language, or in a language only slightly 'heightened' from the normal. There was another poem that used to be one of his favourites, which he used to boom out with a (to me at least) disturbing vocative. 'Nymph' (thunderous low voice), 'Give me your beads!' This, I think, has not entered the anthologies, or at least only a small number of anthologies.

The respected editorial directions are, or proposition is, that Monro's work 'did on the whole steadily improve up to the last (which is a poem in *The Criterion* of a few months ago), that it has a character which clearly distinguishes it both from the Georgian work on the one hand and our own on the other and finally that he received very little appreciation in his lifetime either for the poetry or for his social work'.

Those are the words of authority. I am not an authority, I am but a loathed disturber; but my memory covers a period of Monro's life inaccessible to the Editor,[1] and from it I have attempted to draw certain explanations of causes.

I might question various words in the editorial dictum. They occur in a private letter and the Editor would probably define them more closely were he writing this essay:

'clearly distinguishes'?

Yes, the poems are distinguished from the Georgian, and what distinguishes them is Harold's tendency to 'know it five years after being told'. He was not an

[1] *The Criterion*, July 1932.

wholly closed mind, and the whole tendency of his testament or anthology shows that he gradually came to believe the advance guard, his tendency is steadily toward a definite image and clear speaking in a contemporary idiom. He never abandoned a moral urge (using the term not in an aesthetically pejorative sense). He did not, in 1912, immediately cotton to the fact that a presented image might be the perfectly adequate expression or exposition of *any* urge, whatsoever its nature.

There is need for a lot of dissociation in the terminology relative to image and symbol. The confusion probably arises from using the term symbol as a whole series of ambiguous homophones.

Symbol—an implication of unconventionalized fact or idea.

Symbol—an implication of a *conventionalized* connotation, i.e., as hardly more than a metaphor, or metaphorical expression.

Secondly

'our own'

Here we find a term really needing definition.

I doubt if there is any 'character' *clearly* distinguishing Monro's work from a good deal of mine or even from H. D.'s, there is a different personality personally behind it, but 'character' as an aesthetic term, implying definite clear stylistic demarcation, there quite possibly is not.

'Our own' is too generous a term. And it might be of more general, critical service to point out how a few of 'us' have survived from a pre-Eliot decade, how few

of the people who were there at all, in 1911, would still
be admitted to Mr Eliot's 'our own'.

Our Editor displayed great tact, or enjoyed good
fortune, in arriving in London at a particular date with
a formed style of his own. He also participated in a
movement to which no name has ever been given.

That is to say, at a particular date in a particular room,
two authors, neither engaged in picking the other's
pocket, decided that the dilutation of *vers libre*, Amyg-
ism, Lee Masterism, general floppiness had gone too
far and that some counter-current must be set going.
Parallel situation centuries ago in China. Remedy pre-
scribed 'Émaux et Camées' (or the Bay State Hymn
Book). Rhyme and regular strophes.

Results: Poems in Mr Eliot's *second* volume, not
contained in his first ('Prufrock', *Egoist*, 1917), also
'H. S. Mauberley'.

Divergence later.

Monro's work shows influence of this action, only
once or twice and in a negligible degree. The effects of
the action are usually held to be visible in 'Mr Eliot's
disciples'.

I should be inclined to say Monro's work (so far as
I know it) is *clearly* distinguishable from work related
to the above 'action'.

I doubt if it is clearly distinguished by '*character*' from
all the work in Eliot's first 'Prufrock' or from a good
deal of my own, both before and after the period of
break (vorticism; 1917, etc.). I should be inclined to
think that it is disjunct from that part of 'ours' rather
by personal colouring, personal modification than by
any very clear categoric division of craft. A matter of

degree rather than of kind. There is a far deeper element in some of Eliot's later work to which Monro's best seems more akin.

All of which could be flatly contradicted by unfairly isolating 'The Nightingale near the House', the first poem of Monro's in his own anthology, and evidently one of those he most wished to be judged by. This is in the wholly traditional vein. The 'Midnight Lamentation'[1] is simple and sincere, but also in the general tone of the reflective descriptive essay.

With the fragment from 'The Trees' one comes on what I suppose Mr Eliot calls the 'character', and what one must at any rate agree is the 'personal quality', a certain weight, a certain immediacy of *his* impression, his own simile (elaborated and, alas, described) but indubitably poetic matter contained in its expression if not absolutely coterminous with it.

Indubitably the writer is poet *dans son fort intérieur*, here is 'the stuff of poetry', and in a form that only the very fewest critics can *with any consistency* carp at. I should say that the general reader has no right whatsoever to carp. Probably only those very few fellow-writers who are fortunate or unfortunate enough to have something very like fanatical convictions re métier 'should' investigate or are in any way qualified to undertake anatomization.

We find a sensation or a profound intuition described, described with very great beauty. Only a disbelief in description; a dissociation of description from presentation will provide an excluding category.

Monro's humanity is indisputably present in:

[1] First published. *Chapbook*, 1924.

HAROLD MONRO

'Hearthstone (1915)

I want nothing but your fireside now.
Friend, you are sitting there alone I know,
And the quiet flames are licking up the soot,
Or crackling out of some enormous root:
All the logs on your hearth are four feet long.
Everything in your room is wide and strong
According to the breed of your hard thought.
Now you are leaning forward; you have caught
That great dog by his paw and are holding it,
And he looks sidelong at you, stretching a bit.'

'Strange Companion', 'Trees', touch, characteristic-
ally, the sombre, reach toward the macabre (on this side
more akin to T. S. E.) centre of the personal variant.
Confused, perhaps, a little during period of the later
Yeats, a dark animism, an attribution of moral qualities
to inanimate objects.

During the course of his life—during that of his
literary career—the fashions changed from Stephen
Phillips to Eliot. Harold was not responsible for changes,
his work improved perhaps only as the fashions improved. His last and probably 'best' poem is nearer to
preceding poems by Eliot than to his own 'Paradise'—
on the other hand, he did, I think, maintain something
essentially his own throughout the process (a quarter of
a century long). He did not adopt a fashion for the sake
of adopting a fashion, he persistently resisted and ultimately refused or rejected fashions that were not in
accord with his own content—a content that attains
unencumbered objectivity in *The Criterion's* October
poem ('Bitter Sanctuary'). *Valeat.*

Mr HOUSMAN
AT LITTLE BETHEL[1]

This volume[2] reaches me with a friend's note stating that it has 'upset a lot of the Cambridge critics'. My first hope was, naturally, that the upset had occurred in the highest possible seas and at furthest possible from any danger of rescue.

A. E. H., with consummate caution, takes the ground that he is incompetent to discuss the subject and defies Zeus and Thersites to dislodge him therefrom. So far so good, I might be the last to raise an objection; it is only on page 8 that the eyebrow of the reader tends almost irresistibly to rise: 'The artifice of versification...little explored by critics' (that's true enough), 'a few pages of C. Patmore and F. Myers contain all, so far as I know, or all of value, which has been written on such matters; and to these I could add a few more.'

As autobiography one cannot question the first statement, and as Mr Housman refrains from the adumbrated 'adding' one has no means of knowing whether he be launched into vain jactancy or merely stating a fact.

The marvel is, or would be to any foreigner unacquainted with England, that any professor of Latin in a recognized institution of learning, or any man

[1] The *Criterion*, January 1934.
[2] *The Name and Nature of Poetry*.

alleging that his 'favourite recreation has been the best literature of several languages', could rest for the twenty-two years of his professorate in that phase of 'so far as I know'. Perhaps they have overworked him; left him scant time for his predilected recreation.

He is an ally of righteousness when he alleges that 'good literature read for pleasure must. . . do some good to the reader, quicken his perception. . . sharpen discrimination. . . mellow rawness of personal opinion'.

This bit of dog sense has I suppose upset the clique of critics of critics, who take the ground that Jojo's opinion of Jimjim's explanation of Shakespeare will shed greater light on the reader and initiate him to a higher degree of perception than would perusal of the Bard's original text.

My initial and thirty-year-old divergence from both their houses being that as long as the British critic is damn ignorant of so much of the best literature and even of half a dozen *kinds* of the best literature, English critical writing will be limited in its scope and unsatisfactory not only to the serious writer, but to the reader whose pleasure has been taken in further uplands, or in more wide-lying pastures.

During the twenty-five years wherein my acquaintance with letters has been anything but casual and my observance of English production far from disinterested, I have barged into no single indication that Mr Housman was aware of the world of my contemporaries. That is natural enough, and few men in any country cast a very thoughtful eye on their successors. But even among the writers of Housman's day there must have been a stray hint, a line here and there in, say, the gentle murmurs of

Bridges or Hopkins that could have been added to the
wisdom of Patmore, or to the astuteness of Fred Myers
(whose verse, if any, is unknown to me). None of it, so
far as I know, appears in the worst accepted anthologies,
nor has it been edited by Mr Housman.

I could, if Mr Housman is interested, supply him with
a list of works, which if not specifically catalogued as
'treatises on metric', 'prosody taught in ten lessons',
'tiny tots' guide to the muses', would at least supply him
with an idea here or there, not that I want to impinge
on any man's recreation.

All of which doesn't diminish the fact that Housman's
note in fine print on page 8 is one of the most masterly
summaries of a small section of the problems of metric
that I have ever had the pleasure to come on. I doubt if
anyone has done anything better in English, that is to say,
listed a larger number of more important—some of them
possibly fundamental—issues, in so small a compass.

The marvel is that he should have been willing to rest
on Myers and Patmore. Specific doubt rises with
Housman's specific examples of presumably particular
triumph. Why, for example, are we 'ceasing to gallop
with Callender's horse and beginning to fly with
Pegasus' (like astripitent eagles, etc.) when we come on
a verse writ to the following measure, easier almost to
parody than to transcribe?

> 'Come, tumtum Greek, Ulysses, come[1]
>   Caress these shores with me:
> The windblown seas have wet my bum
>   And here the beer is free.'

[1] Or 'tum' as the case may be.

No! While Dr Bridges' actual verse does not always leap with the springbok, buck with the mustang, course lightly with the gay gazelle, or in any way fill the chest with 'surge and thunder'; and while Gerard Hopkins does not by habit vary his movement with the change of what one would expect to be the underlying emotion, I cannot believe that either Bridges or Hopkins would have been wholly content with Housman's selected illustration.

Mr Housman's prose proceeds with a suavity which the present writer is perfectly willing to envy. Only a biased judgment would deny this, and only a man writing in irritation would, it seems to me, be unaware. One goes from contrast to contrast, Mr Housman's well-known competence up to a point, and the surprising and sudden limits of his cognizance; were he a yokel or yellow press hack, there would be no surprise that he quotes Johnson as the source of J.'s repetition of Aristotle; but from a professor of Latin, a reader, for recreation, of 'several languages'? Ah well, Aristotle was a Greek?

And as for 'the dawn in russet mantle', which is a perfectly good example of the Aristotle via Johnson's 'hall mark of genius', I fail utterly to see *why* it should give only a pleasure purely intellectual and intellectually frivolous, and be of no more virtue than an anagram.

Perhaps the suavity of Housman's writing is not co-partner with precision of thought.

On page 19 I would offer an emendation. As the text stands we are invited to suppose that 'the intelligence' (they are discussing the eighteenth century) involved 'some repressing and silencing of poetry'.

The intelligence never did anything of the sort. (Ref. 'Donne ch' avete intelletto d' amore', 'Voi ch' intendendo il terzo ciel movete', or the pawky comments of Homer!)

The particular form of abstract statement, Voltairian (out of Bayle, out of Quevedo, out of antiquity) kind of reduction *ad absurdum*, etc., dear to the eighteenth century, had an effect on verse. They had no ideogrammic method or hadn't erected it into a system and hadn't heard about Professor Agassiz's fish, but to confuse a tendency to abstract general statement with *tout bonnement* 'intelligence' is to sin against all those most admirable canons of nomenclature which Mr Housman has just so (on his preceding two pages) eulogized.

'The poetry of the eighteenth century,' says Mr Housman, 'was most satisfactory when it did not try to be poetical.' And in other centuries? Again we find a curious trilogy 'satire, controversy and burlesque'. What has satire done, that it should be found so confounded? And what did Hermes say to Calypso?

Mr Housman must be being hortatory, we must indeed be headed for the loftiest possible heights where Homer, Ovid, Dante and Chaucer are not to be quite given the entrée. His bethel must be contracting.

'La pointe de la pyramide,' says Brancusi, 'on est là, on ne peut pas bouger.'

Housman's remark on 'great parsimony and tact' perhaps covers him. If the samples of nineteenth and eighteenth century faded prettiness (on page 22) are to be graded, I candidly doubt whether the latter is inferior to the former. Content more or less kiff/kiff and the eighteenth-century metric rather cleaner?

The general trend of Housman's sermon on the un-
desirability of confusing poetry with 'lofty thoughts
expressed in beeyeewteeful and flowery langwidg', can
however confer nothing save benefit on his readers.
I suppose by 'eighteenth century' he means that century
in England.

Again the pedant in me (who am not like Mr Housman a professor with honours, benefice, ecclesiastical
preferments) arises on a matter of nomenclature.
Housman has dragged in an 'eighteenth century' which
he defines as a condition and not a chronological measure,
and for this extension of language he can find plenty of
justification, though it be just a little off the stipulated
colour of his doctrine.

But is it well found? Dryden, according to my
dictionary of dates, breathed between 1631 and 1700,
Crabbe between 1754 and 1832.

I have never told anyone to read Dryden, who seems
to be the chief and anti-Eliotic demon in Professor
Housman's cosmos, but was Crabbe up till the forty-
sixth year of his age an eighteenth-century writer by
chronology or by spiritual definition? and wasn't Landor
even well into the woollier days of Queen Victoria, not
only by the chronology of his adolescence, but by
affinity with Mr Housman's own definition?

Again the ways of Housman's mind are recondite;
having damned burlesque and disparaged Gilpin as
lacking sublimity, he produces:

'Uprose the sun and up rose Emily'

as Chaucerian unbetterableness. Heaven knows I don't
want to improve it, but is it the height of seriousness,

22

here attained, or have we Chaucerian chuckle? Or at any rate can the reader familiar with Chaucer, but without looking up the context, suppose this line to be any more expressive, any closer to the heart of another's dark forest, etc., than some line of spitfire Alex?

Heaven be my witness that I, at any rate, and of all men, don't want Johnnie Dryden dug up again. Whether by maturity of wit, or whether it be that from early, very early, childhood I have been protected by the association of ideas inherent in the first syllable of John's patronymic —Mr Eliot's endeavours having served only to strengthen my resolve never, never again, to open either John Dryden, his works or any comment upon them, but if anything could stir an interest in that outstanding aridity it would be the isolation and display of some quite sensible remark about Chaucer illustrated pro and con; con by three brays as blatant as Milton; and pro? well, perhaps not very successfully.

In short, Dryden found a rather good critical term, but being by nature a lunk-head, was unable to derive much light from that accident. The marvel, to me, is how any man bent on recreation 'among the best', and yet having so limited a range (apparently) in his selected reading matter, should between beer and the hedgerows have pervaded, transgressed, wandered into, even to the extent of so many quoted lines, Mr Dryden's plasterings upon Chaucer.

On the other hand, Mr Housman has obviously been protected by Heaven. The curse of Isaiah which he shudders to think *had* fallen in the dim years of the treaty of Utrecht, has fairly deluged his country during the literary regencies of Marsh and Abercrombie

(1910 to 1930), and Mr Housman has heard nothing about it.

And the North Pole said to the South Pole: 'Heteroclite is man and there is surely room for a great deal of difference.'

Anyone who can write such neat suave sentences as Mr Housman with such open sincerity is a blessing to... oh, to the present reader—if only to come bang up against another point of view so alien to any preconception, and of a so antipodal difference of disposition.

'No truth', says Housman, 'too precious, observation too profound, sentiment too exalted to be expressed in prose.'

I am unqualified to speak of exalted sentiment, but I should say no idea worth carrying in the mind from one year's end to another, and no story really good enough to make me at least want to tell it, but chafes at the flatness of prose, but suffers from inadequate statement, but leaves me feeling it is but half said, or said in abstraction, defined in terms so elastic that any god's ape can stretch its definition to meet his own squalor or to fit his own imbecility, until it be conjoined with music, or at least given rhythmic definition even though one do not arrive at defining its tonal articulation.

As for 'some ideas do, some do not', etc., Mr Housman is being too 'choosey'. Not the idea but the degree of its definition determines its aptitude for reaching to music.

We have obviously come to a parting of the ways: 'If poetry has a meaning it may be inadvisable to draw it out', *Housman*; 'The intellectual love of a thing consists in the understanding of its perfections', *Spinoza*.

Also 'le style c'est l'homme', *vir quidem*, who may for all I care have been the whole of Latinity, the Mediterranean Everyman, made verb and articulate.

On page 38, Mr Housman descends to bathos, slop, ambiguity, word-twisting, and is like to finish off the respect one had been feeling for him. If the Greek word there translated means 'madness' in the sense of Smart's and Collins' and Willie Blake's being occasionally sent off to do a week-end in an asylum; if it means anything more than a certain tenseness of emotion, a mental excess, no more insane than the kind of physical excess that enabled black Siki to dance back to back with his opponent in a boxing ring, delivering blows over his head, or that enables the sabre ant to cut up a spider, then Plato was an hog, an ape, the louse of a louse, an unprincipled impertinent liar, cutting loose from all the known facts of Greek poetry, none of whose great makers were either lunatics, moon-chewers, village idiots, or general imbeciles, nor were the best Latins, nor was Dante, nor Guido, nor Villon, nor Gautier, Corbière, Browning; and Mr Housman can pack that sentimental drool in his squiffer, and turn his skill to throwing the dart in the pub next adjacent.

Saxpence reward for any authenticated case of intellect having stopped a chap's writing poesy! You might as well claim that railway tracks stop the engine. No one ever claimed they would make it go.

The worship of the village idiot is perhaps peculiar to England? Even the Irish prefer to think the man's mind exists somewhere, though it be gone to the fairies.

When it comes to Shakespeare writing 'nonsense', or to the given example: A. The sample is by no means nonsense. B. The intellect has been in plenary function, Shakespeare being the greatest English technician bar none, and having had the wit to concentrate his technique where the most enlightened intellect would naturally concentrate *technique*, namely on the arrangement of his *sounds*, on the twenty-six letters of his alphabet, on the quality and duration of his syllables and on the varying weights of his accent, pillaging the Italian song books. I mean those of poems printed *with* the music rather than the pages of mere print alone.

The greatest technician, the true English writer of Epos, daring the disparate material of the Histories, again using his *mind*! It took the donkey-eared Milton to pass on that drivelling imbecility about woodnotes so dear to the Wordsworthian epiglottis.

To admire some of Blake's metric you have to forget Lewis Carroll.

That there was a fountain of poetry somewhere inside dippy William, I would be the last to refute, but that the furies and the surges gain by being presented in the dialect of

'Tiger, Tiger, catch 'em quick!
All the little lambs are sick,'

I am mildly inclined to deny. Mr Housman hereabouts is discussing how poetic the that which isn't intellect becomes when expressed in incommensurate language.

I seem to recall something of Herrick's which loses nothing by its author's having been lucid:

'Your dew drink offerings on my tomb'

or something of that sort.

I suspect that Mr Housman suffers from a deficient

curiosity. Such as he has seems hardly to have led him to consider any verse save that having good heavy swat on every alternate syllable, or at least formed predominantly on the system of *ti Tum ti Tum ti Tum*, sometimes up to ten syllables.

On page 47 our author goes down, deeply down, to that jocularity expected of men holding academic honours, and feeling a need to unbend, to meet, to mingle humanly with their audience. Rats, terriers, the 'bristling' of Mr Housman's skin under the razor, if a poetic thought darts through his memory, and last but not Keast, Fanny Brawne!

Milton thou should'st be living at this hour![1]

[1] Meaning that he might have lectured at Cambridge.

HELL[1]

I have always mistrusted Ronsard's boast of having read the *Iliad* in three days, though he might have scuttered through Salel in that time. As a stunt I also might possibly have burrowed through Binyon's version[2] in similar period had it been printed in type decently large.

I state that I have read the work, that for thirty years it never would have occurred to me that it would be possible to read a translation of the *Inferno* from cover to cover, and that this translation has therefore one DEMONSTRATED dimension, whatever may be left to personal taste of the reader or conjecture of acrid critics.

Fools have their uses, and had it not been for the professorial pomp of Mr Wubb or whatever his name is, I might not have found the volume. Mr Wubb leapt upon Binyon's opening triad of lines and managed to display such complete ignorance of the nature of Dantescan verse, and at the same time so thoroughly indicated at least one virtue of Binyon's work that I was aroused to wonder if the venerable Binyon had been able to keep on at that pace.

The venerable Binyon has, I am glad to say, produced the most interesting English version of Dante that I have

[1] *The Criterion*, April 1934.
[2] *Dante's Inferno translated into English Triple Rhyme*, by Laurence Binyon (Macmillan).

seen or expect to see, though I remain in a considerable obscurity as to how far he knows what he has done, and how far he intended the specific results perceptible to the present examiner.

The younger generation may have forgotten Binyon's sad youth, poisoned in the cradle by the abominable dogbiscuit of Milton's rhetoric. I found our translator in 1908 among very leaden Greeks, and in youthful eagerness I descended on the British Museum and perused, it now seems, in retrospect, for days the tales of...demme if I remember anything but a word, one name, Penthesilea, and that not from reading it, but from hearing it spoken by a precocious Binyonian offspring. MR BINYON'S ODE, poster of, was it THE EVENING STANDARD 'Milton Thou should'st', or whatever it was. 'Of Virtuous sire egregious offspring great!'

At any rate Dante has cured him. If ever demonstration be needed of the virtues of having a good model instead of a rhetorical bustuous rumpus, the life in Binyon's translation can prove it to next century's schoolboys.

Mr B. says in preface that he wanted to produce a poem that could be read with pleasure in English. He has carefully preserved all the faults of his original.

This in the circumstances is the most useful thing he could have done. There are already 400 translations of Dante carefully presenting the English reader with a set of faults alien to the original, and therefore of no possible use to the serious reader who wants to understand Dante.

Ninety per cent of the extant versions erect (as Eliot has remarked of G. Murray) 'between the reader and the original a barrier more impassable than the Greek language'.

FIRST: Mr Binyon has not offered us a pre-Raphaelite version of Dante.

Note that even Shadwell in his delicate renderings of cantos 26 to 33 of the *Purgatorio* has given us something not Dante, he has given us something that might almost have started from *Aucassin and Nicolette*, so far as the actual feel and texture of the work is concerned. He has taken the most fragile frosting and filagree, to begin on, he started, if my memory serves me, with that particular part of the *Commedia*, and gradually went on to the rest, or at least first to the *Purgatorio* and then to the *Paradiso*, with great delicacy of expression.

I propose to deal with our present translator very severely. He is himself a dour man, with all the marginalia of the Commonwealth. You could dress him and pass him off for one of Noll's troopers, and though he be my elder in years, I am, if his preface means what I think it does, his senior in the struggle with early Italian verse.

I cannot imagine any serious writer being satisfied with his own work in this field, or indeed any serious writer being satisfied with his own product in this field or in any other.

If Binyon has been on this job for twelve years, I have been on it or in its environs for three and twenty or longer. Twenty-eight might be more exact. However drasticly I hack at the present translation, I warn the rash novice that I can probably make a fool of any other critic who rushes in without similar preparation.

Irritated by Binyon's writing his lines hind side before, with the verbs stuck out of place on the tail syllable, and with multiple relative clauses, I (somewhere along about canto VI) wondered if it was worth while showing up the defects in Dante, especia ly as it seems probable that no one since Savage Landor would have been capable of weighing them. Weighing them, that is, justly, and in proportion to the specific force of the WHOLE POEM.

Heaven knows critical sense has not abounded in Italy.

Dante's Inferno Part One
'Culture and Refinement'
(*Kensington cinema billboard, a.d.* 1915)

The devil of translating medieval poetry into English is that it is very hard to decide HOW you are to render work done with one set of criteria in a language NOW subject to different criteria.

Translate the church of St Hilaire of Poitiers into Barocco?

You can't, as anyone knows, translate it into English of the period. The Plantagenet Kings' Provençal was Langue d'Oc.

Latin word order obeyed the laws for dynamics of inflected language, but in 1190 and in 1300, the language of the highbrows was still very greatly Latin. The concept of word order in uninflected or very little inflected language had not developed to anything like twentieth-century straightness. Binyon makes a very courageous statement, and a sound one: 'melodious smoothness is not the characteristic of Dante's verse.'

Despite Sordello's mastery and the ingenuity of Ar. Daniel, despite Dante's Provençal studies and the melody of his own lyrics, and despite the tremendous music of the *Commedia*, Dante, in taking up narrative, chucked out a number of MINOR criteria, as any writer of a long poem must in favour of a main virtue, and that main virtue Binyon (willing or not meaning to) has possibly exaggerated. At any rate it is now possible to READ the 34 Canti. . .*as a continuity*.

There is no danger that the reader will be intoxicated at any one point, and lulled into delight with the sound, as he may quite well be even with the original.

Binyon is in the fortunate position of not having to introduce his poet, he doesn't have to resurrect him, or gain attention for him. Here he is with one of the three greatest reputations in all literature. Anyone who don't know the *Commedia* is thereby ignoramus. It is not to be expected that I can honestly care very much how it strikes the new reader.

If, after all these years, I have read straight through the *Inferno*, and if, after all my previous voyages over that text, and even efforts to help the less trained, I have now a clearer conception of the *Inferno as a whole* than I had the week before last, that is a debt, and not one that I mean to be tardy in paying.

> 'The love of a thing consists in the understanding of its perfections.' (Spinoza.)

Spinoza's statement distinctly includes knowing what they (the perfections) are NOT. Mr Binyon has not offered a lollypop, neither did Dante. *Pensi lettor!*

The habit of a degraded criticism is to criticize all, or most books, as if all books were written with the same aim. The old teachers of dialectic knew better (*Ut moveat, ut doceat ut delectet*).

Dante wrote his poem to MAKE PEOPLE THINK, just as definitely as Swinburne wrote a good deal of his poetry to tear the pants off the Victorian era and to replace the Albert Memorial by Lampascus.

The style for a poem written to that end, or in translation of same, differs from the style suited to a 3000 dollar magazine story in the wake of de Maupassant.

PROSODY

I have never seen but one intelligent essay on Dante's 'metre', and that was in an out-of-print school-book found in a Sicilian hotel, the author cited an author who had examined Dante's actual practice and found that the 'eleven syllable' line was composed of various different syllable-groups, totalling roughly eleven syllables, and not running, so far as I can remember, to more than seventeen. Any pedant can verify the top limit, and it doesn't greatly matter so long as the student does not confuse the so-called 'syllabic' system with 'English pentameter', meaning a swat at syllables, 2, 4, 6, 8, 10 in each line, mitigated by 'irregularities' and 'inverted feet'.

Mr Wubb had apparently *not* heard of the difference, at the time of his objection to Binyon. There is nothing in Binyon's own preface to indicate that he himself had it clearly in mind as a 'concept'. He does not refer to the *De Volgari Eloquio*. It wouldn't surprise me if he had read it and forgotten it (more or less), but a man can't be immured for forty years with Koyets' and Sotatz' without developing some sort of sensibility to outline and demarcation, and without learning to distinguish muddy from clear; neither can he go on reading Dante for twelve years with the serious intention of finding an English equivalent without perceiving at least SOME of the qualities of the SOUND of the original, whether or no he invent a 'system' or theory for explaining that sound.

SHIFT:

I remember Yeats wanting me to speak some verse aloud in the old out-of-door Greek theàtre at Siracusa, and being annoyed when I bellowed the

ποικιλόθρον, ἀθάνατ' Αφρόδιτα

and refused to spout English poesy. I don't know how far I succeeded in convincing him that English verse wasn't CUT. Yeats himself in his early work produced marvellous rhythmic effects 'legato', verse, that is, very fine to murmur and that may be understood if whispered in a drawing-room, even though the better readers may gradually pull the words out of shape (by excessive lengthening of the vowel sounds).

The musical terms 'staccato' and 'legato' apply to verse. The common verse of Britain from 1890 to 1910 was a horrible agglomerate compost, not minted, most of it not even baked, all legato, a doughy mess of third-hand Keats, Wordsworth, heaven knows what, fourth-hand Elizabethan sonority blunted, half melted, lumpy. The Elizabethan 'iambic' verse was largely made to bawl in theatres, and had considerable affinity with barocco.

Working on a decent basis, Binyon has got rid of pseudo-magniloquence, of puffed words, I don't re-member a single decorative or rhetorical word in his

first ten cantos. There are vast numbers of mono-
syllables, little words. Here a hint from the *De Eloquio*
may have put him on the trail.

In the matter of rhyme, nearly everyone knows that
Dante's rhymes are 'feminine', i.e. accent on the pen-
ultimate, *crucciata, aguzza, volge, maligno*. There are
feminine rhymes in English, there are ENOUGH, possibly, to fill the needs of an almost literal version of the
Divina Commedia, but they are of the wrong quality;
bloweth, knowing, waiteth.

Binyon has very intelligently avoided a mere pseudo
or obvious similarity, in favour of a fundamental,
namely the sharp clear quality of the original SOUND
as a whole. His *past, admits, checked, kings*, all masculine
endings, but all leaving a residue of vowel sound in state
of potential, or latent, as considered by Dante himself
in his remarks on troubadour verse.

I do not expect to see another version as good as
Binyon's, I can to a great extent risk being unjust to forty
translators whose work I haven't seen. Few men of
Binyon's position and experience have tried or will try
the experiment. You cannot counterfeit forty years'
honest work, or get the same result by being a clever
young man who prefers vanilla to orange or heliotrope
to lavender perfume.

'La sculpture n'est pas pour les jeunes hommes'
(Brancusi.)

A younger generation, or at least a younger American
generation, has been brought up on a list of acid tests,
invented to get rid of the boiled oatmeal consistency of
the bad verse of 1900, and there is no doubt that many

young readers seeing Binyon's inversions, etc., will be likely to throw down the translation under the impression that it is incompetent.

The fact that this idiom, which was never spoken on sea or land, is NOT fit for use in the new poetry of 1933–4 does not mean that it is unfit for use in a translation of a poem finished in 1321.

Before flying to the conclusion that certain things are 'against the rules' (heaven save us, procedures are already erected into RULES!) let the neophyte consider that a man cannot be in New York and Pekin at the same moment. Certain qualities are in OPPOSITION to others, water cannot exist as water and as ice at the same time.

It WOULD be quite possible to conserve the natural word order, without giving up the rhymes used by Binyon, IF one used run-on instead of end-stopped verses. BUT Dante's verses are mostly end-stopped. Various alternatives are offered at every juncture, but let the neophyte try half a dozen before deciding that Binyon has sacrificed the greater virtue for the less in a given case.

He has not made such sacrifice in his refusal to bother with feminine rhyme. Specific passages must be judged line by line. And this process I propose to illustrate by particular cases before falling into general statement.

In a poem 200 pages long, or more exactly in a poem the first third of which is 200 pages long, the FIRST requirement is that the reader be able to proceed. You can't do this with Chapman's *Homer*. You plunge into adjectival magnificence and get stuck. You have two or more pages of admiration, and then wait to regather your energies, or you acquire a definite impression of Chapman's language, and very little of Ilion. There are even, and this is more pertinent, a great number of persons familiar with the Paolo and Francesca incident, and very muzzy about the *Commedia* as a Whole.

Literature belongs to no one man, and translations of great works ought perhaps to be made by a committee. We are cut off (by idiotic economic system), etc. from the old habit of commentary printed WITH a text. Up to canto VIII or IX I was torn between wanting Binyon to spend the next ten years revising his *Inferno*, and the wish he should go on to the end of the *Commedia*, and then, if he had time, turn back for revision. I now think he has earned his right to the pleasures of the *Purgatorio* and the third section of the poem. Some, perhaps most of the strictures made on particular passages, might better be made privately to the translator were there such opportunity or any likelihood that my opinion would be well received. It is nearly impossible to make the RIGHT suggestion for emending another man's work. Even if you do, he never quite thinks it remains his own. This ulcerated sense of property might disappear in an ideal republic. At most, one can put one's finger on the fault and hope the man himself will receive inspiration from the depths of his own personal Helicon.

> *Dante's Inferno Part Two*
> 'Not a Dull Moment'.
>
> (*Kensington billboard*)

If any of the following citations seem trifling or carping let the reader think how few contemporary works merit *in any degree* this sort of attention.

For most translation one would merely say, take it away and start again. There is nothing in the following list that couldn't be dealt with in a second or third edition.

An imaginary opponent might argue that Binyon had given us 'penny plain' for 'twopence coloured'. Sargent used to do coloured impressions of Velasquez, but so far as I know he didn't try the process on Dürer. If Binyon has given us an engraving, he has put the original in its own colour on the opposite page.

If the opponent think Binyon somewhat naïf not to try to hide the defects of Dante, this also has its use and its interest, at least as preparation for understanding subsequent Italy. At last one sees what Petrarch was trying to get away from, and why the Italians have put up with Petrarch.

Minor triumph, in 1932: I drove an Italian critic, author of a seven volume history of Italian literature, to his last ditch, whence he finally defended Petrarch on the sole ground that 'one occasionally likes a chocolate cream'. A literary decadence can proceed not only from a bad colossal author, but from a small man's trying to avoid the defects in the work of a great man.

Returning from relative to intrinsic value: We owe Binyon a great debt for having shown (let us hope once and for all) how little Dante needs NOTES. The general lay reader has been hypnotized for centuries by the critical apparatus of the *Commedia*. An edition like Moore's with no notes, especially if approached by a young student, is too difficult. One was thankful in 1906 to Dent for the Temple bilingual edition, it saved one from consulting Witte, Toynbee, God knows whom, but at any rate from painfully digging in with a dictionary, a Dante dictionary, etc....and one (I believe MORE—I cannot believe my experience unique) never got through to the essential fact that it is really THERE ON THE PAGE.

One got interested in the wealth of heteroclite material, incident, heteroclite anecdote, museum of mediæval history, etc. Whenever there was an immediate difficulty one looked at a note, instead of reading on for ten lines and waiting for Dante to tell one.

Binyon's canto headings average about half a page. Up to canto XIII I can think of only one item necessary, or at least that one wanted, for the understanding of the text, which he hasn't included in his summaries.

This is really an enormous benefit, a very great work of clearance and drainage. And it ought not to pass without gratitude. It is partly due to this clearance that the version leaves one so clear headed as to the general line of the Cantico.

At the start the constant syntactical inversions annoy one. Later one gets used to the idiom and forgets to notice them. In any case there is nothing worse than Dante's own:

> 'già mai non vada,
> di là più che di qua essere aspetta.'

There are however during the first dozen cantos a number of alterations from singular to plural, or vice versa, which do no good whatever.

In the main Binyon's having his eye on the word and not the thing makes for the honesty of the version, or transparency in the sense that one sees through TO the original. Later the translator gets his eye on the object without losing grip on the verbal manifestation.

MINUTIA: Canto I, *freckled* not very good for *gaetta*.

III. Not having worked into the idiom one is annoyed by inversions and extra words. Shadwell, if I remember rightly, tried an eight syllable line to get a weight equal to the Italian. I don't know that anyone has thought of attempting the poem in terza rima, but with fewer English lines than the Italian. It would breed, probably, considerable confusion, it might cause a denseness that would defeat the main end: penetrability.

III. 134, *crimson* for *vermiglia*, given the context this is Binyon's worst oversight, or in strict sense *lack* of sight.

Canto V. *Inspects*, good. *I mean* for *dico*, excellent. *Scrutinize*, excellent; *row on row*, excellent and not literal. *Desire* and *Reason*, with caps, a little out of style; *rapt in air*, excellent.

And comest journeying through the black air, good. *Caina* is Cain's hell, rather than *place*.

VI, line 3, *which* (printer's error?), l. 28, faint Miltonism. *Muddy* for *tinta*, good.

For thou wast made before I was unmade, good.

VII, *from class to class*, modern and not trecento. But very interesting as lyric insertion from the translator. Certain glints or side lights, have value as comment.

IX. I don't know that it is necessary to assume that Dante's Medusa is the strictly classical female. Bunting has perhaps pierced deeper with his 'Come, we'll enamel him'. Enamel is both stone and fusing heat. Frogs don't *run* through water. Not quite sure re *spaldi*, it is a *gallery*; I dare say it might be a closed gallery under *battlements* (as at Assisi).

X. I don't think *slaughterous* helps; *nato* has gender, and would allow *son* as equivalent.

XI. *Of all malice*, passage, rather modern in attitude, not quite the *odio in cielo acquista.*

XII. Excellent example Binyon's understanding of the difference between the Dantescan line and English 'pentameter':

> *Running as in the world once they were wont.*

There is an excellent slight distortion making for greater vividness and forcing the reader to think more about the exact meaning of the original in:

> *Who live by violence and on other's fear.*

On the next page, a very clear example of quality of motion in the original

> *che mori per la bella Deianira.*

Figliastro, usually *step* son (printer's error?).

XIII, *fosco*, dark, and *schietto* not so much smooth as *clean* or *straightish*; *polsi*, both *wrists* and *vigour*; *becomes the grain*, excellent and the kind of thing Dante liked.

XIV, *tames* for *maturi*, not so felicitous.

l. 92. Dante's metaphor (*pasto*) about all the traffic will stand, but to *seek light*, as well as to have *taste vouchedsafe* is 'uno di piu'.

XV, *avventa*? sea forced in by the wind; *nervi*, a word one could wrangle over; *fiera*, possibly more *proud* than *fierce*.

This minor contentiousness is not impertinent if it emphasize the progressive tightening of poet's attention from Homer to Ovid, to Dante. Dürer's grasshopper in the foreground will serve for visual comparison. Dürer is about the most helpful source for optical suggestion that I can think of. One might also note the almost uninterrupted decadence of writers' attention for centuries after Dante, until the gradual struggle back toward it in Crabbe, Stendhal, Browning and Flaubert.

XVIII. Coming back again to the rhyming, not only are we without strict English feminine equivalents for terminal sounds like *ferrigno*, *rintoppa*, *argento*, *tronca*, *stagna*, *feruto*, but any attempt at ornamental rhyme would be out of place, any attempt at explosive rhyme à la Hudibras, or slick epigrammatic rhyme à la Pope or trick rhyme à la Hood, or in fact any kind of rhyming excresence or ornament would be out of place in the *Commedia*, where Dante's rhyme is but a stiffer thread in the texture, to keep the whole from sprawling and pulling out of trim shape (cf. weave of any high grade trouser material).

One advantage of having the book in penetrable idiom is that we (one, I) see more clearly the grading of Dante's values, and especially how the whole hell reeks with money. The usurers are there as against nature, against the natural increase of agriculture or of any productive work.

Deep hell is reached via Geryon (fraud) of the marvellous patterned hide, and for ten cantos thereafter the damned are all of them damned for money.

The filth heaped upon Thais seems excessive, and Binyon here might have given us a note indicating the gulf between Francesca, or Rahab, and the female who persuaded Alexander to burn the Palace of Persepolis.

The allusive bit of conversation doesn't explain this, though I suppose it occurs in whatever account Dante knew.

Dante's morals are almost sovietic in his location of the grafters who are lower down than even the simonists. The English term barrator has been, I think, reserved for translations of Dante and occurs nowhere else outside the dictionary, the present legal sense being either different or specialized. *Baro* is a cheater at cards, in Italian, and *grafter* is the exact equivalent of *barattier*, and if grafter is now a neologism, there are, despite Dante's theorizing about aulic speech, several unparliamentary and uncurial terms in this section of the *Inferno*. Meaning betrayer of public trust, the term is more exact than one used explicitly of appropriation of vessels at sea. The word has applied to so many members of the social register, so many multi-millionaires, American presidents, French cabinet ministers, that it will probably have social if not literary status henceforward.

XX. Whether anyone has noted the Spanish sound at the end of this canto, I don't know, it is possibly a parallel for Arnaut's passage in Provençal in the *Purgatorio* (Sobilia, ? Sibilia, nocque, introcque).

XXV. These low circles are not for simple carnality, the damned here have always a strong stain of meanness, cheating though not, I admit, brought into strong relief: *fraudulent* homicide, Cacus for 'furto *frodolente*'. It begins with the usurers in canto XI. We have lost the mediæval discrimination between productive and destructive investment, as we have lost the idea decay of intelligence re/*ben del intelletto*.

Though Dante's sense of main construction is perhaps

rudimentary in comparison with Flaubert's, one might note definite parallels, or stays, tending toward general shape, apart from the diagrammatic or cartographic scheme, e.g. the Spanish suggestion, Ciampolo (XXII) against the honest Romeo, Agnel in the Ovidian metamorphosis (*due e nessun*) vs. Bertrand (*ed uno in due*).

The punishment of prophets and soothsayers seems overdone, but 'wax image witchcraft' is the clue, or at any rate the link between Dante's attitude and our own, a common basis for revulsion.

(XX, 123). 'Fecer malie con erbe e con imago'

(XXV, 97.) 'Nor Ovid more of Arethusa sing,
                    To water turned, or Cadmus to a snake.'

I give this alternative to show how easy it is to get a couple of word for word lines of smooth and liquid versification that are utterly un-Dantescan and translate much less than Binyon's contortion.

After a comparatively dull stretch, canto XXV imposes Dante's adjunct, the profounder metamorphosis of the nature (soul) agglutinous fluidity, and he calls specific attention to it, and to the fact that he is adding something not in Lucan and Ovid. In fact after Guido and Dante, whatever there may have been in human mind and perception, literature does not again make any very serious attempt to enter these regions of consciousness till almost our own day, in the struggles of Henry James and of Ibsen (who has passed out of fad and not yet come back into due currency). (Even Donne and Co. were engaged in something rather different.)

XXVI, moment of inattention 'winging the heavenly vault' is nonsense, not in the original, out of place.

Re punishment of Ulysses, no one seems to note the perfectly useless, trifling unprovoked sack of the Cicones in the *Odyssey*. Troy was one thing, they were inveigled.

Helen's father was trying to dodge destiny by a clever combination, etc., but for the sack of the Ciconian town there was no excuse handy, it is pure devilment, and Ulysses and Co. deserved all they got thereafter (not that there is any certainty that Dante had this in mind).

It gives a crime and punishment motif to the *Odyssey*, which is frequently overlooked, and is promptly and (?) properly snowed under by the human interest in Odysseus himself, the live man among duds. Dante definitely accents the theft of the Palladium, whereon one could turn out a volume of comment. It binds through from Homer to Virgil to Dante.

XXVI. Supposing this to be the first segment the translator attempted, his later work shows very considerable progress, and a much more vigorous grasp on his matter.

From here on there are one or two slack passages a matter of a line or two, there are a few extra words and there are compensations as in XXVIII, *plow still disinters* being more specific than *accoglie*, *camminata* is *corridor* rather than *chamber*, and *burella* a *pit-shaft*. One ends with gratitude for demonstration that forty years' honest work do, after all, count for something; that some qualities of writing cannot be attained simply by clever faking, young muscles or a desire to get somewhere in a hurry.

The lines move to their end, that is, draw along the eye of the reader, instead of cradling him in a hammock. The main import is not sacrificed to detail. Simple as this appears in bald statement, it takes time to learn how to achieve it.

2

'WE HAVE HAD NO BATTLES
BUT WE HAVE ALL JOINED
IN AND MADE ROADS'

I take this line from a letter of Capt. Goldoni's to indicate the new *forma mentis* with a date line 1935. The three essays preceding this interlude can be taken as retrospect; the three which follow, as gropings which were not retrospective when written, and which must now be taken in perspective.

No man who is building anything more than a suburban villa can be expected to have his construction always on the market, always finished, with all the scaffoldings taken down. In the dim mainly forgotten backward of 1908 and 1910 a few men in London groped toward the 'revolution of the word'. Collectors of wash-lists finding rags now on every midden have begun reconstructions, which cannot greatly enlighten mankind.

At 50 one cannot make any complete statement without reference to details already set in order. 'Ut doceat, ut moveat, ut delectet.' This classification I got from a certain Agricola, who presumably had it of antiquity. Without this 'in partes tres' I see no very sane criticism.

'Doceat, moveat' should be fused in the delectet in any great work of art. Separate, they belong to action and as action they pass in time, with the day or the hour contingent. The need of teaching goes when the scholar has learned, the need of moving, with the mass action intended. But begun at the wrong end or hind end, the delectet is prone to mean mere literature of escape.

The revolution of the word began so far as it affected the men who were of my age in London in 1908, with the LONE whimper of Ford Madox Hueffer. His more pliant disciples were Flint, Goldring, and D. H. Lawrence. Hueffer (Ford) read Flaubert and Maupassant in a way that George Moore did not. Impressionism meant for him something it did not to Mr Symons.

The cleaning up of the WORD had not got down to orthology or the severities we now read into that term. Aestheticism had not spared wholly our brother. It took Yeats and Symons one way, and Bro. Ford another. Nevertheless the literary historian will err if he tries to start the 'revolution of the word' a decade or so later with the emergence of Mr Joyce's epigons and jejune admirers. Hueffer's (Ford's) succession is not in the new gongorism but in orthology, where I think Mr Ford will dislike it.

Simultaneously and independently (or even precedently, though I think not) Fenollosa was learning from Prof. Mori and Umewaka Minoru. The rise of the CORPORATE ideal ran parallel with the composition of 'The Chinese Written Character'.

WHENCE the new forma mentis. At Fenollosa's death in 1908 his essay was indubitably ahead of its time. How far, may be judged by the bestial incomprehension it met with when I finally jammed it into print ten and bit more years later. The number of people now fit to read it will perhaps be gauged by the sales of the reprint.

A new mode of thought was foreseen. A mode that would eliminate certain types of imbecility, in particular the inaccessibility to FACT glaringly lit up in 1935 by the peril of world conflagration caused by the type of mind which festered in the ideologues of the Wilson-Angell congregation. Bad writing could have been taken as symptom of the European disease.

Bad writing, or a great deal of it, drips down from an abstract received 'idea' or 'generality' held with fanaticism (twin beast with personal vanity) by men who NEVER take in concrete detail.

Men are good or bad in the year 1935 in proportion as they will LOOK AT the facts, new facts, any facts.

That is part of the new FORMA MENTIS. Forma to the great minds of at least one epoch meant something more than dead pattern or fixed opinion. 'The light of the DOER, as it were a form cleaving to it' meant an ACTIVE pattern, a pattern that set things in motion.

(This sentence can be taken along with my comment on Guido and in particular the end of the chapter called 'Mediævalism'.)

Here we approach the ideal 'corporate'. McNair Wilson, following one clear book by another, has I think seen war as 'contingent'. I think he has seen Europe as Whole. In this present light booklet I am, by request, keeping OFF economics and politics; but I cannot touch even the edges of literature without asserting once again, the UNIVERSALITY of the word. That is specific in my *A.B.C. of Reading* and in earlier drafts of what I have said there.

The WORD built out of perception of COMPONENT parts of its meaning reaches down and through and out into all ethics and politics. Clean the word, clearly define its borders and health pervades the whole human congeries, *in una parte più e meno altrove*.

The Latin ideal, as ideal, has its place in the new congeries. Whether that ideal be defined by public man or by a private observer. The dispassionate reader will not reject the implications of my quoted title. There is an unsympathetic Italian author named G. Ferrero who 35 years ago was writing about the plough as conquistador. Until the literary reader has an at least as nearly total perception of the world he lives in as had McNair Wilson when he wrote *Defeat of Debt*, I fail to see how he is going to perceive the 'Histoire Morale Contemporaine' in action or even to recognize it after some real writer has written it down.

War is CONTINGENT; even dictatorship is contingent. Both depend on usura and ignorance. Dictatorship is not in our time a word current in Italy. The idea here is leadership.

It may be that my weekly writings are no more articulate than the trumpetings of a terrified elephant. I have no specific will to preserve them as written. The elephant's noise serves a purpose: to warn its contingent herd. The proportion of indignation to fear in any animal cry must be judged by its musical qualities, as one judges cities by their sound and their feel.

The weight of any mental onrush can be gauged only by something resistant. If the lesser cattle all pell mell flee to avoid the impact, one has no exact measure of its physical energy. Clamantis deserto, I find it very difficult to find an opponent. This I state without any vanity. It may be due to defects of style. Only from concurrents do I receive any real correction. Butchart, Angold, Jeffry Mark, McNair Wilson help me correct my deflections. Time and again I have to rectify my angles of error, or put in the missing components. But from the liary of the 'other side' these corrections are N O T forthcoming. No one corrected my definition of capital. It was not *wrong*, it was insufficient. I had to find the further dissociation, and boundary.

A S F O R T H E R E V O L U T I O N of the *word*. It makes no difference whether we are writing of money or landscapes. Madox Ford's aim toward the just word was right in his personal circle of reference. He was dealing mainly with visual and oral perceptions, whereinto come only colours, concrete forms, tones of voice, modes of gesture.

O U T of these you build sane ideogram. You build your congeries, in validity.

Ogden's trailers having read only, or mainly, textbooks fail lamentably when they come to giving examples. They even write about literature in a painful unacquaintance of the great books.

As example of where language gets to when you leave it prey to the profit motive, I offer the following axes of reference: (1) *L'art industriel* and M. Arnoux as analysed in Flaubert's *Éducation Sentimentale*, (2) the unconscious and comic echo of Arnoux by a league of nations female mystic met in a Roman park (Nov. anno quattordici), and (3) the passing word of an art dealer. I treasure my art dealers. I so rarely meet one. This one was loose on a quai in Venice. Wondering where the market had got to, I asked what he dealt in, and what he could sell in New York. His reply came with perfect slickness, and from an immeasurable sense of superiority, simplex munditiis, he answered unhesitant: 'The best.'

This meant, as I found, very expensive canvasses of recognized masters. It included NO work by unrecognized men. On that point he was specific. He just couldn't handle 'em. Quality of the work made no difference. This I adduce not as means of pinching the baby or getting dollars for impecunious artists, but as evidence re the meaning of a word (a top bracket adjective).

The word, rotted by commerce, affects us all where we live. It has built up a set of counterfeit 'idealists' who jeopard every man's life, mind, and food. For the purpose of this booklet, let us keep to the segment 'mind'. No man short of attaining supreme wisdom can WELCOME facts against his own case with the same joy that receives confirmations.

Nevertheless my complaint against the massed opposition is that they steadily refuse to bring up ANY facts whatsoever. They bring up parrot cries, verbal curley-cues which EXCLUDE the known facts. When those facts were literary facts, specific works or distinguished writers, one could leave one's writing in a corner, in the left turret of anyone's ivory tower. When these facts menace the good life in totality one is less disposed to sit by, making cat's cradles. Et voilà l'histoire de mon petit frère, che son' io. In a world menaced by destruction from PERCEIVABLE conscious and half-conscious and unconscious people and forces, in a world wherein a new leaven is working ALL OVER THE PLACE, a lavender pervaded retrospect is less absorbing than when one was learning one's métier from preceding example.

UT delectet. The first caressings of pleasure are possibly not goads. I have written, thinking of *narrative* prose that it can only be best done in indifference, when one can hardly be bothered to put word after word.

It may even be that the serene flow of sentence is more exciting to the reader than are words set down in anger. But when one is not narrating? when one specifies the new life or the new temple? When one talks to the capo maestro, that is to the building foreman as distinct from making architectural pictures that one knows will remain for ever (or for ages) unrealized, one may have other criteria? Risking the END of the reader's interest when the house or palace is up?

(And an now my deerly beeluvved brevvrem etc. et cetera.)

     ★   ★   ★   ★   ★

I have, and more than once, been specificly asked not to write about economics. Even as I sit here an editor accuses me of writing Italian propaganda. I am no more writing Italian propaganda than is the calm McNair Wilson. I am writing for humanity in a world eaten by usury. I write for a cultural heritage that includes centuries of anti-usurious doctrine and results thereof in cathedral building. *Usura* was a moral issue, it was a religious issue. It is still an ethical issue, and religious wherever religion merits a name. Even a dexterous, perhaps over dexterous banker defined to me the distinction between partaggio and usura as a moral distinction.

'WE HAVE HAD NO BATTLES'

When men will neither look at fact nor read the Ta Hio, it is difficult to write to them about letters (pure letters, etc.). I shall be told that the next three essays are unconvincing but that is implicit in my title. Polite essays are not printed to convince anyone of anything whatsoever. The next few pages must be taken as record of what I saw when I wrote them. They must stand as chronicle, without which what I write now would probably be seen out of focus.

6 Dec. anno XIV

THE PROSE TRADITION IN VERSE [1]

In a country in love with amateurs, in a country where the incompetent have such beautiful manners, and personalities so fragile and charming, that one cannot bear to injure their feelings by the introduction of competent criticism, it is well that one man should have a vision of perfection and that he should be sick to the death and disconsolate because he cannot attain it.

Mr Yeats wrote years ago that the highest poetry is so precious that one should be willing to search many a dull tome to find and gather the fragments. As touching poetry this was, perhaps, no new feeling. Yet where nearly everyone else is still dominated by an eighteenth-century verbalism, Mr Hueffer has had this instinct for prose. It is he who has insisted, in the face of a still Victorian press, upon the importance of good writing as opposed to the opalescent word, the rhetorical tradition. Stendhal had said, and Flaubert, de Maupassant and Turgenev had proved, that 'prose was the higher art'—at least their prose.

Of course it is impossible to talk about perfection without getting yourself very much disliked. It is even more difficult in a capital where everybody's Aunt Lucy or Uncle George has written something or other, and where the victory of any standard save that of mediocrity

[1] *Poetry* (Chicago), 1914.

would at once banish so many nice people from the temple of immortality. So it comes about that Mr Hueffer is the best critic in England, one might say the only critic of any importance. What he says to-day the press, the reviewers, who hate him and who disparage his books, will say in about nine years' time, or possibly sooner. Shelley, Yeats, Swinburne, with their 'unacknowledged legislators', with 'Nothing affects these people except our conversation', with 'The rest live under us'; Remy de Gourmont, when he says that most men think only husks and shells of the thoughts that have been already lived over by others, have shown their very just appreciation of the system of echoes, of the general vacuity of public opinion. America is like England, America is very much what England would be with the two hundred most interesting people removed. One's life is the score of this two hundred with whom one happens to have made friends. I do not see that we need to say the rest live under them, but it is certain that what these people say comes to pass. They live in their mutual credence, and thus they live things over and fashion them before the rest of the world is aware. I dare say it is a Cassandra-like and useless faculty, at least from the world's point of view. Mr Hueffer has possessed the peculiar faculty of 'foresight', or of constructive criticism, in a pre-eminent degree. Real power will run any machine. Mr Hueffer said fifteen years ago that a certain unknown Bonar Law would lead the conservative party. Five years ago he said with equal impartiality that D. H. Lawrence would write notable prose, that Mr de la Mare could write verses, and that *Chance* would make Conrad popular.

Of course if you think things ten or fifteen or twenty years before anyone else thinks them you will be considered absurd and ridiculous. Mr Allen Upward, thinking with great lucidity along very different lines, is still considered absurd. Some professor feels that if certain ideas gain ground he will have to re-write his lectures, some parson feels that if certain other ideas are accepted he will have to throw up his position. They search for the forecaster's weak points.

Mr Hueffer is still underestimated for another reason also: namely, that we have not yet learned that prose is as precious and as much to be sought after as verse, even its hreds and patches. So that, if one of the finest chapters in English is hidden in a claptrap novel, we cannot weigh the vision which made it against the weariness or the confusion which dragged down the rest of the work. Yet we would do this readily with a poem. If a novel have a form as distinct as that of a sonnet, and if its workmanship be as fine as that of some Pleiade rondel, we complain of the slightness of the motive. Yet we would not deny praise to the rondel. So it remains for a prose craftsman like Arnold Bennett to speak well of Mr Hueffer's prose, and for a verse-craftsman like myself to speak well of his verses. And the general public will have little or none of him because he does not put on pontifical robes, because he does not take up the megaphone of some known and accepted pose, and because he makes enemies among the stupid by his rather engaging frankness.

We may as well begin reviewing the *Collected Poems* with the knowledge that Mr Hueffer is a keen critic and a skilled writer of prose, and we may add that he is not wholly unsuccessful as a composer, and that he has given us, in 'On Heaven', the best poem yet written in the 'twentieth-century fashion'.

I drag in these apparently extraneous matters in order to focus attention on certain phases of significance, which might otherwise escape the hurried reader in a volume where the actual achievement is uneven. Coleridge has spoken of 'the miracle that might be wrought simply by one man's feeling a thing more clearly or more poignantly than anyone had felt it before'. The last century showed us a fair example when Swinburne awoke to the fact that poetry was an art, not merely a vehicle for the propagation of doctrine. England and Germany are still showing the effects of his perception. I cannot belittle my belief that Mr Hueffer's realization that poetry should be written at least as well as prose will have as wide a result. He himself will tell you that it is 'all Christina Rossetti', and that 'it was not Wordsworth', for Wordsworth was so busied about the ordinary word that he never found time to think about *le mot juste*.

As for Christina, Mr Hueffer is a better critic than I am, and I would be the last to deny that a certain limpidity and precision are the ultimate qualities of style; yet I cannot accept his opinion. Christina had these qualities, it is true—in places, but they are to be found also in Browning and even in Swinburne at rare moments. Christina very often sets my teeth on edge—and so for that matter does Mr Hueffer. But it is the function of criticism to find what a given work is, rather than what it is not. It is also the faculty of a capital or of high civilization to value a man for some rare ability, to make use of him and not hinder him or itself by asking of him faculties which he does not possess.

Mr Hueffer may have found certain properties of style first, for himself, in Christina, but others have found them elsewhere, notably in Arnaut Daniel and in Guido and in Dante, where Christina herself would have found them. Still there is no denying that there is less of the *ore rotundo* in Christina's work than in that of her contemporaries, and that there is also in Hueffer's writing a clear descent from such passages as:

> 'I listened to their honest chat:
>> Said one: "To-morrow we shall be
> Plod plod along the featureless sands
>> And coasting miles and miles of sea."
> Said one: "Before the turn of tide
>> We will achieve the eyrie-seat."
> Said one: "To-morrow shall be like
>> To-day, but much more sweet."'

We find the qualities of what some people are calling 'the modern cadence' in this strophe, also in 'A Dirge', in 'Up Hill', in—

> 'Somewhere or other there must surely be
> The face not seen, the voice not heard,'

and in—

> 'Sometimes I said: "It is an empty name
>> I long for; to a name why should I give
> The peace of all the days I have to live?"—
>> Yet gave it all the same.'

Mr Hueffer brings to his work a prose training such as Christina never had, and it is absolutely the devil to try to quote snippets from a man whose poems are gracious impressions, leisurely, low-toned. One would quote 'The Starling', but one would have to give the whole three pages of it. And one would like to quote patches out of the curious medley, 'To All the Dead'— save that the picturesque patches aren't the whole or the feel of it; or Sussmund's capricious 'Address', a sort of 'Inferno' to the 'Heaven' which we are printing for the first time in another part of this issue. But that also is too long, so I content myself with the opening of an earlier poem, 'Finchley Road'.

> 'As we come up at Baker Street
> Where tubes and trains and 'buses meet
> There's a touch of fog and a touch of sleet;
> And we go on up Hampstead way
> Toward the closing in of day....
>
> You should be a queen or a duchess rather,
> Reigning, instead of a warlike father,
> In peaceful times o'er a tiny town,
> Where all the roads wind up and down
> From your little palace—a small, old place
> Where every soul should know your face
> And bless your coming.'

I quote again, from a still earlier poem where the quiet of his manner is less marked:

> 'Being in Rome I wonder will you go
>   Up to the Hill. But I forget the name...
> Aventine? Pincio? No: I do not know
>   I was there yesterday and watched. You came.'

(*I give the opening only to 'place' the second portion of the poem.*)

62

'Though you're in Rome you will not go, my You,
Up to that Hill...but I forget the name.
Aventine? Pincio? No, I never knew...
I was there yesterday. You never came.

I have that Rome; and you, you have a Me,
You have a Rome, and I, I have my You;
My Rome is not your Rome: my You, not you.
              ......For, if man knew woman
I should have plumbed your heart; if woman, man,
Your Me should be true I...If in your day—
You who have mingled with my soul in dreams,
You who have given my life an aim and purpose,
A heart, an imaged form—if in your dreams
You have imagined unfamiliar cities
And me among them, I shall never stand
Beneath your pillars or your poplar groves,...
Images, simulacra, towns of dreams
That never march upon each other's borders,
And bring no comfort to each other's hearts!'

I present this passage, not because it is an example of
Mr Hueffer's no longer reminiscent style, but because,
like much that appeared four years ago in 'Songs from
London', or earlier still in 'From Inland', it hangs in my
memory. And so little modern work does hang in one's
memory, and these books created so little excitement
when they appeared. One took them as a matter of
course, and they're not a matter of course, and still less
is the later work a matter of course. Oh well, you all
remember the preface to the collected poems with its
passage about the Shepherd's Bush exhibition, for it
appeared first as a pair of essays in *Poetry*, so there is

no need for me to speak further of Mr Hueffer's aims or of his prose, or of his power to render an impression.

There is in his work another phase that depends somewhat upon his knowledge of instrumental music. Dante has defined a poem as a composition of words set to music, and the intelligent critic will demand that either the composition of words or the music shall possess a certain interest, or that there be some aptitude in their jointure together. It is true that since Dante's day—and indeed his day and Casella's saw a re-beginning of it—'music' and 'poetry' have drifted apart, and we have had a third thing which is called 'word music'. I mean we have poems which are read or even, in a fashion, intoned, and are 'musical' in some sort of complete or inclusive sense that makes it impossible or inadvisable to 'set them to music'. I mean obviously such poems as the First Chorus of 'Atalanta' or many of Mr Yeats' lyrics. The words have a music of their own, and a second 'musician's' music is an impertinence or an intrusion.

There still remains the song to sing: to be 'set to music', and of this sort of poem Mr Hueffer has given us notable examples in his rendering of Von der Vogelweide's 'Tandaradei' and, in lighter measure, in his own 'The Three-Ten':

'When in the prime and May-day time dead lovers went a-walking,
How bright the grass in lads' eyes was, how easy poet's talking!
Here were green hills and daffodils, and copses to contain them:
Daisies for floors did front their doors agog for maids to chain them.

64

So when the ray of rising day did pierce the eastern
    heaven

Maids did arise to make the skies seem brighter far by
    seven.

Now here's a street where 'bus routes meet, and 'twixt
    the wheels and paving

Standeth a lout who doth hold out flowers not worth
    the having.

But see, but see! The clock strikes three above the Kilburn
    Station,

Those maids, thank God, are 'neath the sod and all their
    generation.

What she shall wear who'll soon appear, it is not hood
    nor wimple,

But by the powers there are no flowers so stately or
    so simple.

And paper shops and full 'bus tops confront the sun
    so brightly,

That, come three-ten, no lovers then had hearts that
    beat so lightly

As ours or loved more truly,

Or found green shades or flowered glades to fit their
    loves more duly.

And see, and see! 'Tis ten past three above the Kilburn
    Station,

Those maids, thank God! are 'neath the sod and all their
    generation.'

Oh well, there are very few song writers in England,
and it's a simple old-fashioned song with a note of
futurism in its very lyric refrain; and I dare say you will
pay as little attention to it as I did five years ago. And

if you sing it aloud, once over, to yourself, I dare say you'll be just as incapable of getting it out of your head, which is perhaps one test of a lyric.

It is not, however, for Mr Hueffer's gift of song-writing that I have reviewed him at such length; this gift is rare but not novel. I find him significant and revolutionary because of his insistence upon clarity and precision, upon the prose tradition; in brief, upon efficient writing—even in verse.

DR WILLIAMS' POSITION[1]

I

There is an anecdote told me by his mother, who wished me to understand his character, as follows: The young William Carlos, aged let us say about seven, arose in the morning, dressed and put on his shoes. Both shoes buttoned on the left side. He regarded this untoward phenomenon for a few moments and then carefully removed the shoes, placed shoe *a* that had been on his left foot, on his right foot, and shoe *b*, that had been on the right foot, on his left foot; both sets of buttons again appeared on the left side of the shoes.

This stumped him. With the shoes so buttoned he went to school, but...and here is the significant part of the story, he spent the day in careful consideration of the matter.

It happens that this type of sensibility, persisting through forty years, is of extreme, and almost unique, value in a land teeming with clever people, all capable of competent and almost instantaneous extroversion; during the last twenty of these years it has distinguished Dr Williams from the floral and unconscious minds of the populace and from the snappy go-getters who'der seen wot wuz rong in er moment.

It has prevented our author from grabbing ready

[1] *Dial*, Nov. 1928.

67

made conclusions, and from taking too much for granted.

There are perhaps, or perhaps have been milieux where the reflective and examining habits would not have conferred, unsupported, a distinction. But chez nous, for as long as I can remember if an article appeared in Munsey's or McClure's, expressing a noble passion (civic or other) one could bank (supposing one were exercising editorial or quasi-editorial functions) on seeing the same article served up again in some fifty lyric expressions within, let us say, three or four months.

Our national mind hath about it something 'marvellous porous'; an idea or notion dropped into New York harbour emerges in Santa Fé or Galveston, watered, diluted, but still the same idea or notion, pale but not wholly denatured; and the time of transit is very considerably lower, than any 'record' hitherto known. We have the defects of our qualities, and that very alertness which makes the single American diverting or enlivening in an European assembly often undermines his literary capacity.

For fifteen or eighteen years I have cited Williams as sole known American-dwelling author who could be counted on to oppose some sort of barrier to such penetration; the sole catalectic in whose presence some sort of modification would take place.

Williams has written: 'All I do is to try to understand something in its natural colours and shapes.' There could be no better effort underlying any literary process, or used as preparative for literary process; but it appears, it would seem, almost incomprehensible to men dwelling west of the Atlantic: I don't mean that it appears so in theory, America will swallow anything in theory, all abstract statements are perfectly welcome, given a sufficiently plausible turn. But the concrete example of this literary process, whether by Williams or by that still more unreceived and uncomprehended native hickory Mr Joseph Gould, seems an unrelated and inexplicable incident to our populace and to our 'monde—or whatever it is—littéraire'. We have, of course, distinctly American authors, Mr Frost for example, but there is an infinite gulf between Mr Frost on New England customs, and Mr Gould on race prejudice; Mr Frost having simply taken on, without any apparent self-questioning a definite type and set of ideas and sensibilities, known and established in his ancestral demesne. That is to say he is 'typical New England'. Gould is no less New England, but parts of his writing could have proceeded equally well from a Russian, a German, or an exceptional Frenchman—the difference between regionalism, or regionalist art and art that has its root in a given locality.

Carlos Williams has been determined to stand or sit as an American. Freud would probably say 'because his father was English' (in fact half English, half Danish). His mother, as ethnologists have before noted, was a mixture of French and Spanish; of late years (the last four or five) Dr Williams has laid claim to a somewhat remote Hebrew connexion, possibly a rabbi in Saragossa, at the time of the siege. He claims American birth, but I strongly suspect that he emerged on shipboard just off Bedloe's Island and that his dark and serious eyes gazed up in their first sober contemplation at the Statue and its brazen and monstrous nightshirt.

At any rate he has not in his ancestral endocrines the arid curse of our nation. None of his immediate forbears burnt witches in Salem, or attended assemblies for producing prohibitions. His father was in the rum trade; the rich ichors of the Indes, Hollands, Jamaicas, Goldwasser, Curaçoas provided the infant William with material sustenance. Spanish was not a strange tongue, and the trade profited by discrimination, by dissociations performed with the palate. All of which belongs to an American yesterday, and is as gone as les caves de Mouquin.

From this secure ingle William Carlos was able to look out on his circumjacence and see it as something interesting *but exterior*; and he could not by any possibility resemble any member of the Concord School. He was able to observe national phenomena without necessity for constant vigilance over himself, there was no instinctive fear that if he forgot himself he might be like some really unpleasant Ralph Waldo; neither is he, apparently, filled with any vivid desire to murder the indescribable dastards who betray the work of the national founders, who spread the fish-hooks of bureaucracy in our once, perhaps, pleasant bypaths.

One might accuse him of being, blessedly, the observant foreigner, perceiving American vegetation and landscape quite directly, as something put there for him to look at; and this contemplative habit extends, also blessedly, to the fauna.

When Mr Wanamaker's picture gallery burned in the dead of winter I was able to observe the destruction of faked Van Dykes, etc., *comme spectacle*, the muffler'd lads of the village tearing down gold frames in the light of the conflagration, the onyx-topped tables against the blackness were still more 'tableau', and one could think detachedly of the French Revolution. Mr Wanamaker was nothing to me, he paid his employees badly, and I knew the actual spectacle was all I should ever get out of him. I cannot, on the other hand, observe the nation befouled by Volsteads and Bryans, without anger; I cannot see liberties that have lasted for a century thrown away for nothing, for worse than nothing, for slop; frontiers tied up by an imbecile bureaucracy exceeding 'anything known in Russia under the Czars' without indignation.[1]

And by just this susceptibility on my part Williams, as author, has the no small advantage. If he wants to 'do' anything about what he sees, this desire for action does not rise until he has meditated in full and at leisure. Where I see scoundrels and vandals, he sees a spectacle or an ineluctable process of nature. Where I want to kill at once, he ruminates, and if this rumination leads to anger it is an almost inarticulate anger, that may but lend colour to style, but which stays almost wholly in the realm of his art. I mean it is a qualificative, contemplative, does not drive him to some ultra-artistic or non-artistic activity.

Even recently where one of his characters clearly expresses a dissatisfaction with the American milieu, it is an odium against a condition of mind, not against overt acts or institutions.

[1] This comparison to Russia is not mine, but comes from a Czarist official who had been stationed in Washington.

2

The lack of celerity in his process, the unfamiliarity with facile or with established solutions would account for the irritation his earlier prose, as I remember it, caused to sophisticated Britons. 'How any man could go on talking about such things!' and so on. But the results of this sobriety of unhurried contemplation, when apparent in such a book as *The American Grain*, equally account for the immediate appreciation of Williams by the small number of French critics whose culture is sufficiently wide to permit them to read any modern tongue save their own.

Here, at last, was an America treated with a seriousness and by a process comprehensible to an European.

One might say that Williams has but one fixed idea, as an author; i.e., he starts where an European would start if an European were about to write of America: sic: America is a subject of interest, one must inspect it, analyse it, and treat it as subject. There are plenty of people who think they 'ought' to write 'about' America. This is an wholly different kettle of fish. There are also numerous people who think that the given subject has an inherent interest simply because it is American and that this gives it ipso facto a dignity or value above all other possible subjects; Williams may even think he has, or may once have thought he had this angle of attack, but he hasn't.

After a number of years, and apropos of a given incident he has (first quarterly number of *Transition*) given a perfectly clear verbal manifestation of his critical attitude. It is that of his most worthy European contemporaries, and of all good critics. It is also symptomatic of New York that his analysis of the so-called criticisms of Antheil's New York concert should appear in Paris, a year after the event, in an amateur periodical.

The main point of his article being that no single one of the critics had made the least attempt at analysis, or had in any way tried to tell the reader what the music consisted of, what were its modes or procedures. And that this was, of course, what the critics were, or would in any civilized country have been, there for. This article is perhaps Williams' most important, or at any rate most apposite, piece of critical writing, failing a wide distribution of the magazine in which it appeared, it should be reprinted in some more widely distributable journal.

It would seem that the illusion of 'progress' is limited, chez nous, to the greater prevalence of erotic adventure, whether developed in quality or merely increased in quantity I have no present means of deciding; the illusion as to any corresponding 'progress' or catching-up in affairs of the intellect, would seem to rise from the fact that in our literary milieux certain things are now known that were not known in 1912; but this does not constitute a change of relation; i.e. does not prove that America is not still fifteen years or twenty years or more 'behind the times'. We must breed a non-Mabie, non-Howells type of author. And of the possible types Williams and Gould serve as our best examples—as distinct from the porous types.

I mean, not by this sentence, but by the whole trend of this article: when a creative act occurs in America 'no one' seems aware of what is occurring. In music we have chefs d'orchestre, not composers, and we have something very like it in letters, though the distinction is less obvious.

Following this metaphor, it is undeniable that part of my time, for example, has been put into orchestral directing. Very little of Dr Williams' energy has been so deflected. If he did some Rimbaud forty years late it was nevertheless composition, and I don't think he knew it was Rimbaud until after he finished his operation.

Orchestral directing is 'all right' mais c'est pas la même chose. We are still so generally obsessed by monism and monotheistical backwash, and ideas of orthodoxy that we (and the benighted Britons) can hardly observe a dissociation of ideas without thinking a censure is somehow therein implied.

We are not, of course we are not, free from the errors of post-reformation Europe. The triviality of philosophical writers through the last few centuries is extraordinary, in the extent that is, that they have not profited by modes of thought quite common to biological students; in the extent that they rely on wholly unfounded assumptions, for no more apparent reason than that these assumptions are currently and commonly made. Reputed philosophers will proceed (for volumes at a time) as if the only alternative for monism were dualism; among distinguished literati, si licet, taking personal examples: Mr Joyce will argue for hours as if one's attack on Christianity were an attack on the Roman church *in favour of* Luther or Calvin or some other half-baked ignoramus and the 'protestant' conventicle. Mr Eliot will reply, even in print, to Mr Babbitt as if some form of Christianity or monotheism were the sole alternative to irreligion; and as if monism or monotheism were anything more than an hypothesis agreeable to certain types of very lazy mind too weak to bear an uncertainty or to remain in 'uncertainty'.

And, again, for such reasons William Williams, and may we say, his Mediterranean equipment, has an importance in relation to his temporal intellectual circumjacence.

Very well, he does not 'conclude'; his work has been 'often formless', 'incoherent', opaque, obscure, obfuscated, confused, truncated, etc.

I am not going to say: 'form' is a non-literary component shoved on to literature by Aristotle or by some non-litteratus who told Aristotle about it. Major form is not a non-literary component. But it can do us no harm to stop an hour or so and consider the number of very important chunks of world-literature in which form, major form, is remarkable mainly for absence.

There is a corking plot to the *Iliad*, but it is not told us in the poem, or at least not in the parts of the poem known to history as The Iliad. It would be hard to find a worse justification of the theories of dramatic construction than the *Prometheus* of Aeschylus. It will take a brighter lad than the author of these presents to demonstrate the element of form in Montaigne or in Rabelais; Lope has it, but it is not the 'Aristotelian' beginning, middle and end, it is the quite reprehensible: BEGINNING WHOOP and then any sort of a trail off. *Bouvard and Pécuchet* wasn't even finished by its author. And of all these Lope is the only one we could sacrifice without inestimable loss and impoverishment.

The component of these great works and *the* indispensable component is texture; which Dr Williams indubitably has in the best, and in increasingly frequent, passages of his writing.

3

In current American fiction that has, often, quite a good deal of merit, and which has apparently been concocted with effort and goodish intentions, the failure to attain first-rateness seems to be mainly of two sorts: The post-Zolas or post-realists deal with subject matter, human types, etc., so simple that one is more entertained by Fabre's insects or Hudson's birds and wild animals. The habits or the reactions of 'an ant' or 'a chaffinch' emerge in a more satisfactory purity or at least in some modus that at least seems to present a more firm and sustaining pabulum to reflection.

Secondly: there are the perfumed writers. They aim, one believes, at olde lavender; but the ultimate aroma lacks freshness. 'Stale meringue', 'last week's custard' and other metaphorical expressions leap to mind when one attempts to give an impression of their quality. One 'ought' perhaps to make a closer analysis and give the receipt for the fadeur; though like all mediocre dilutations it is harder to analyse than the clearer and fresher substance. When I was fourteen, people used to read novels of the same sort, let us say *The House of a Thousand Candles*, etc., of which one may remember a title, but never remembers anything else, and of which the author's name has, at the end of five or ten years, escaped one.

It is perfectly natural that people wholly surrounded

by roughnecks, whether in mid-nineteenth century or in The Hesperian present, should want to indicate the desirability of sweetness and refinement, but...these things belong to a different order of existence, different that is from pity, terror, τὸ καλόν, and those things with which art, plastic or that of the writer, is concerned.

Now in reading Williams, let us say this last book *A Voyage to Pagany* or almost anything else he has written, one may often feel: he is wrong. I don't mean wrong in idea, but: that is the wrong way to write it. He oughtn't to have said that. But there is a residue of effect. The work is always distinct from writing that one finds merely hopeless and in strict sense irremediable.

There is a difference in kind between it and the mass of current writing, about which there is just nothing to be done, and which no series of re-touches, or cuttings away would clarify, or leave hard.

Art very possibly *ought* to be the supreme achievement, the 'accomplished'; but there is the other satisfactory effect, that of a man hurling himself at an indomitable chaos, and yanking and hauling as much of it as possible into some sort of order (or beauty), aware of it both as chaos and as potential.

Form is, indeed, very tiresome when in reading current novel, we observe the thinning residue of pages, 50, 30, and realize that there is now only time (space) for the hero to die a violent death, no other solution being feasible in that number of pages.

To come at it another way: There are books that are clever enough, good enough, well enough done to fool the people who don't know, or to divert one in hours of fatigue. There are other books—and they may be often less clever, and may often show less accomplishment—which, despite their ineptitudes, and lack of accomplishment, or 'form', and finish, contain something for the best minds of the time, a time, any time. If *Pagany* is not Williams' best book, if even on some counts, being his first long work, it is his worst, it indubitably contains pages and passages that are worth any one's while, and that provide mental cud for any ruminant tooth.

4

And finally, to comply with those requirements for critics which Dr Williams has outlined in his censure of Mr Antheil's critics: The particular book that is occasion for this general discussion of Williams, *A Voyage to Pagany*,[1] has not very much to do with the 'art of novel writing', which Dr Williams has fairly clearly abjured. Its plot-device is the primitive one of 'a journey', frankly avowed. Entire pages could have found place in a simple autobiography of travel.

In the genealogy of writing it stems from *Ulysses*, or rather we would say better: Williams' *The Great American Novel*, 80 pages, Three Mountains Press, 1923, was Williams' first and strongest derivation from *Ulysses*, an 'inner monologue', stronger and more gnarled, or stronger *because* more gnarled at least as I see it, than the *Pagany*.

The other offspring from *Ulysses*, the only other I have seen possessing any value, is John Rodker's

[1] *A Voyage to Pagany*, by William Carlos Williams (The Macaulay Company, 10mo., 338 pages, $2.50).

Adolphe, 1920. The two books are greatly different. *The Great American Novel* is simply the application of Joycean method to the American circumjacence. The *Adolphe*, professedly taking its schema from Benjamin Constant, brings the Joycean methodic inventions into a form; slighter than *Ulysses*, as a rondeau is slighter than a canzone, but indubitably a 'development', a definite step in general progress of writing; having, as have at least two other novels by Rodker, its definite shaped construction. And yet, if one read it often enough, the element of form emerges in *The Great American Novel*, not probably governing the whole, but in the shaping of at least some of the chapters, notably Chapter VII, the one beginning 'Nuevo Mundo'.

As to subject or problem, the *Pagany* relates to the Jamesian problem of U.S.A. *v.* Europe, the international relation, etc.; the particular equation of the Vienna milieu has had recent treatment 'from the other end on' in Joseph Bard's *Shipwreck in Europe*, more sprightly and probably less deeply concerned with the salvation of the protagonist; I think the continental author mentions as a general and known post-war quantity: the American or Americans who comes or come to Vienna to find out why they can't enjoy life, even after getting a great deal of money.

The American Grain remains, I imagine, Dr Williams' book having the greater interest for the European reader. In the looseish structure of the *Pagany* I don't quite make out what, unless it be simple vagary of the printer, has caused the omission of 'The Venus' (July *Dial*), pages obviously written to occur somewhere in the longer work, though they do form a whole in themselves, and pose quite clearly the general question, or at least one phase of the question in the *Pagany*.

In all the books cited,[1] the best pages of Williams—at least for the present reviewer—are those where he has made the least effort to fit anything into either story, book, or (*In The American Grain*) into an essay. I would almost move from that isolated instance to the generalization that plot, major form, or outline should be left to authors who feel some inner need for the same; even let us say a very strong, unusual, unescapable need for these things; and to books where the said form, plot, etc., springs naturally from the matter treated. When put on ab exteriore, they probably lead only to dullness, confusion or remplissage or the 'falling between two stools'. I don't mean that Williams 'falls'; he certainly has never loaded on enough shapings to bother one. As to his two dialectical ladies? Of course he may know ladies who argue like that. There may be ladies who so argue, aided by Bacchus. In any case the effect of one human on another is such that Williams may elicit such dialectic from ladies who in presence of a more dialectic or voluble male would be themselves notably less so. No one else now writing would have given us the sharp clarity of the medical chapters.

As to the general value of Carlos Williams' poetry I have nothing to retract from the affirmation of its value that I made ten years ago, nor do I see any

[1] *The Tempers* (Elkin Matthews, 1913); *Al Que Quiere* (The Four Seas Company, 1917); *Kora in Hell* (The Four Seas Company, 1920); *Sour Grapes* (The Four Seas Company, 1921); *The Great American Novel* (Three Mountains Press, 1923); *The American Grain* (Albert and Charles Boni, 1925); *A Voyage to Pagany* (The Macaulay Company, 1928).

particular need of repeating that estimate; I should have to say the same things, and it would be with but a pretence or camouflage of novelty.

When an author preserves, by any means whatsoever, his integrity, I take it we ought to be thankful. We retain a liberty to speculate as to how he might have done better, what paths would conduce to, say progress in his next opus, etc. to ask whether for example Williams would have done better to have read W. H. Hudson than to have been interested in Joyce. At least there is place for reflection as to whether the method of Hudson's *A Traveller in Little Things* would serve for an author so concerned with his own insides as is Williams; or whether Williams himself isn't at his best—retaining interest in the uncommunicable or the hidden roots of the consciousness of people he meets, but confining his statement to presentation of their objective manifests.

No one but a fanatic impressionist or a fanatic subjectivist or introversionist will try to answer such a question save in relation to a given specific work.

JAMES JOYCE ET PÉCUCHET[1]

James Joyce, né à Dublin vers 1882, reçut une éducation catholique, étudia à l'université de Dublin,
passa des années ou des semaines à Paris et à Padoue,
se fit, à Dublin, une réputation d'"excentrique", débuta
en 1908, avec *Chamber Music*, une trentaine de pages
de vers conventionnels et délicats, qui montrent l'âme
et la vraie personnalité de cet auteur aujourd'hui si
redouté.

Ce premier livre ne dissipa point le silence; son
deuxième livre, une série de contes intitulée *Dubliners*,
fut brûlé par une main mystérieuse et sa ville natale ne
cessa de se montrer insensible aux mérites de l'auteur.
A Londres, *The Egoist*, revue de cénacle, protesta et
entreprit la publication de son roman: *Portrait of the
Artist as a young Man*, maintenant traduit en suédois, en
espagnol et en français (le volume va paraître sous le
titre *Daedalus*).

Son drame *Exiles* fut joué à Munich, et la traduction
italienne parut dans *Convegno*. L'accueil de Joyce par
ses compatriotes tardait encore à se faire.

L'année du centenaire de Flaubert, première d'une ère
nouvelle, voit aussi l'édition d'un nouveau volume de
Joyce, *Ulysses*, qui, à certains points de vue, peut être
considéré comme le premier qui, en héritant de Flaubert,

[1] *Mercure de France*, 1er Juin, 1922.

continue le développement de l'art flaubertien, tel qu'il l'a laissé dans son dernier livre inachevé.

Bien que *Bouvard et Pécuchet* ne passe pas pour la 'meilleure chose' du maître, on peut soutenir que *Bovary* et l'*Éducation* ne sont que l'apogée d'une forme antérieure; et que les *Trois Contes* donnent une espèce de sommaire de tout ce que Flaubert avait acquis en écrivant ses autres romans, *Salammbô*, *Bovary*, l'*Éducation* et les premières versions de *Saint Antoine*. Les trois tableaux, païen, moyenâgeux, moderne, font un tout qui se balance sur la phrase: 'Et l'idée lui vint d'employer son existence au service des autres', qui se trouve au milieu de *Saint Julien*, le premier des trois contes qu'il écrivit.

Bouvard et Pécuchet continue la pensée et l'art flaubertien, mais ne continue pas cette tradition du roman ou du conte. On peut regarder 'l'Encyclopédie en farce' qui porte en sous-titre: 'Défaut de méthode dans les sciences', comme l'inauguration d'une forme nouvelle, une forme qui n'avait pas son précédent. Ni *Gargantua*, ni *Don Quijote*, ni le *Tristram Shandy* de Sterne n'en avaient donné l'archétype.

Si l'on considère les grandes lignes de la littérature universelle depuis 1880, on peut dire que les meilleurs écrivains ont exploité Flaubert plutôt que développé son art. La règle absolue d'un succès instantané, c'est qu'il ne faut jamais donner à une lectrice un instant, un demi-instant de travail cérébral. Maupassant a fait du Flaubert plus léger; les autres l'ont suivi. Anatole France se sert de Flaubert comme d'une espèce de paravent, et se retire dans son XVIIIe siècle. Galdos, en Espagne, fait du bon Flaubert; Hueffer, en Angleterre, écrit une prose lucide; Joyce, lui-même, dans *Dubliners* et dans *The Portrait of the Artist as a young Man*, fait du Flaubert, mais ne dépasse pas les *Trois Contes* ni l'*Éducation*. Dans l'héritage de Flaubert il y a de bonnes œuvres et une espèce de décadence, les meilleurs disciples emploient les mêmes procédés, les mêmes découvertes techniques pour représenter des scènes différentes; pour décrire les Indes Kipling fait du Maupassant inférieur. En France, Flaubert détient le 'record': personne ne développe son art.

Le développement de Henry James et de Marcel Proust vient plutôt des Goncourt, pas même de leurs romans, mais d'une préface:

'Le jour où l'analyse cruelle que mon ami Zola, et peut-être moi-même avons apporté dans la peinture du bas de la société sera reprise par un écrivain de talent, et employée à la reproduction des hommes et des femmes du monde, dans les milieux d'éducation et de distinction, ce jour-là seulement le classicisme et sa queue seront tués.

'Le Réalisme n'a pas en effet l'unique mission de décrire ce qui est bas, ce qui est répugnant....Nous avons commencé, nous, par la canaille, parce que la femme et l'homme du peuple, plus rapprochés de la nature et de la sauvagerie, sont des créatures simples et peu compliquées, tandis que le Parisien et la Parisienne de la société, ces civilisés excessifs, dont l'originalité tranchée est faite toute de nuances, toute de demi-teintes, tout de ces riens insaisissables, pareils aux riens coquets et neutres avec lesquels se façonne le caractère d'une toilette distinguée de femme, demandent des années pour qu'on les perce, pour qu'on les sache, pour qu'on les *attrape*, et le romancier du plus grand génie, croyez-le bien, ne les devinera jamais, ces gens de salon, avec les *racontars* d'amis qui vont pour lui à la découverte dans le monde.…'

Dans cette voie Henry James a créé la meilleure part de son œuvre, très exacte, très réaliste; et, à la remorque de James, Marcel Proust a clarifié ses intentions, c'est-à-dire qu'il avait commencé par la lecture de Balzac, Dostoïevsky, H. James, ou des œuvres de tendance analogue. Il voyait que l'intérêt 'sexe' dominait et appauvrissait les romans français contemporains. Il comprit qu'il y avait un coin vide dans la littérature française. Il y courut, et sur son pastiche enduisit un vernis de nacre symboliste. Plus tard il épurait son style, et, dans le dîner Guermantien, il ne lui en reste que l'élément qui ressemble à James. En effet, James n'a rien fait de mieux.

Mais ces tableaux de la haute société sont une spécialisation, une arabesque, charmante, intéressante, tant que vous voudrez, plutôt qu'un progrès radical de méthode. Et tout cela correspond dans l'œuvre de Flaubert à *Bovary*, à l'*Éducation*, et au *Cœur Simple*.

Quant aux romans historiques, ils n'ont jamais ressuscité depuis que Laforgue leur lançait ce coup dans l'épigastre: *Salomé*.

Les vrais critiques ne sont pas les juges stériles, les faiseurs de phrases. Le critique efficace est l'artiste qui vient après, pour tuer, ou pour hériter; pour dépasser, pour augmenter, ou pour diminuer et enterrer une forme. Depuis les exactitudes du télescope de *Salomé* on ne s'attaque plus aux détails historiques.

'Il y a même', écrit Remy de Gourmont, 'à la mi-carême, le costume historique.'

A côté de tout cela il y a la Russie, la profondeur un peu alcoolique, ou épileptique, et informe de Dostoïevsky, ses disciples et ses inférieurs; il y a le Strindbergisme et le subjectivisme qui n'offre peut-être rien de plus réussi qu'*Adolphe*.

Mais qu'est-ce que *Bouvard et Pécuchet*? Heureusement le livre de votre plus solide flaubertien, René Descharmes, et les paroles de Flaubert lui-même m'évitent une définition trop 'amateur', trop 'étranger': 'Encyclopédie mise en farce.' (Flaubert soutient, ou a soutenu pour cinq minutes une autre mienne irrévérence; il appelle *La Tentation* une 'ancienne toquade', mais passons.)

Autour de Bouvard et Pécuchet est charmant comme toute œuvre définitive qui ose être 'trop' méticuleuse afin de trancher la question une fois pour toutes, de mettre fin à des blagues, à de vagues pérambulations. Les arguments de M. Descharmes sont tellement solides, les faits qu'il apporte si incontestables que j'ai presque peur de proposer quelques divergences de vue. Mais de temps en temps il employe des phrases qui, sorties de leur contexte, peuvent devenir tendancieuses ou occasionner des malentendus. Je trouve:

'Page 44...des traits de la passion de Frédéric ne revêtent toute leur importance psychologique que si on les rapporte à la passion éprouvée par Flaubert pour Mme Schlesinger.'

Plus tard je me demande ce qu'il entend par 'l'intelligence complète d'une œuvre'.

Il a, peut-être, employé les termes justes. Mais on doit souligner que si on ne comprend pas une œuvre seulement par la lecture de cette œuvre et rien que de cette œuvre, on ne la comprendra jamais; même avec toute la masse de documents, de citations, de détails biologiques ou biographiques que vous voudrez. Tout ce qui n'est pas l'œuvre appartient à la biographie de l'auteur; ce qui est un autre sujet, sujet d'un autre livre réaliste, mais qui n'appartient nullement à 'l'intelligence de l'œuvre' complète ou autre. (J'exagère.)

Il y avait un fait-divers Delamarre; il y avait mille autres faits aussi divers. Flaubert en avait choisi un. Il y avait un vitrail à Reims, à Rouen, une peinture de Breughel à Gênes; tout cela est fort intéressant quand on s'intéresse énormément à cet être intéressant entre tous qu'était Gustave Flaubert; mais le lecteur de *Saint Julien* et de *Bovary* peut s'en ficher de bon cœur. M. Descharmes est presque de mon avis, mais il confine à cet imbécile de Sainte-Beuve,[1] et on a envie alors de crier 'gare!'

Descharmes démontre que l'action de *Bouvard et Pécuchet* est impossible dans le temps donné. Il pose la question de savoir si Flaubert avait l'intention de se passer de son réalisme habituel et de se présenter ses deux bonshommes comme une espèce de prodige doué

---

[1] Sainte-Beuve: Je demande pardon de traiter ainsi un Monsieur qui a son monument au Jardin du Luxembourg avec ceux de Clémence Isaure, Scheurer-Kestner (1833–1899), Fifine de Médicis, Adam, Ève, Rûcher École, et tant d'autres gloires de la race françoise; avec celui de Flaubert lui-même, mais ses arrière-petits-bâtards, c'est-à-dire les arrière-petits-fils de Sainte-Beuve ont tellement empesté le monde Anglo-Saxon, où chaque pignouf, qui n'a aucune aptitude à comprendre une œuvre se met à faire de la critique 'littéraire' en vomissant des paperasses sur les factures de la blanchisseuse de Whitman, la correspondance de Géo. Eliot et sa couturière, etc., etc....que...que Bossuet reste l'Aigle de Meaux.

d'une avant-vieillesse éternelle. C'est un détail qu'une dernière revision aurait pu facilement arranger; un détail, je crois, de l'espèce de ceux qu'on laisse au dernier remaniement.

Descharmes nous présente des recherches fort amusantes sur la mnémotechnie de Feinaigle, et sur la gymnastique d'Amoros. Il fait là une œuvre nouvelle et réaliste. Et il prouve que Flaubert n'a rien exagéré.

Pour *Bouvard et Pécuchet* il ne trouve aucun fait-divers; mais il me semble qu'il y avait à Croisset deux hommes dont l'un au moins avait une curiosité sans borne. Si Flaubert, qui satirise tout, n'a pas satirisé un certain M. Laporte et un certain M. Flaubert bien connus et peu considérés des Rouennois, il est certain qu'il passait sa vie toujours avec 'un autre'; avec Le Poittevin, avec l'erreur Du Camp, avec Bouilhet; rien de plus naturel que cette conception de deux hommes qui font des recherches. Les recherches de Flaubert hors de la littérature n'auraient jamais pu le satisfaire; de là sa sympathie pour ses bonshommes; la vanité de sa propre lutte contre l'imbécillité générale donne de l'énergie au portrait de ces autres victimes des circonstances. La supposition vaut bien les autres qu'on fait dans les analyses chimiques et cliniques des œuvres d'art. Descharmes l'effleure, page 236.

Mais c'est surtout dans le chapitre sur les 'idées reçues' qu'il nous intéresse, et c'est par là qu'on voit un rapport entre Flaubert et Joyce. Entre 1880 et l'année où fut commencé *Ulysses* personne n'a eu le courage de faire le sottisier gigantesque, ni la patience de rechercher l'homme-type, la généralisation la plus générale.

Descharmes établit la différence entre le 'dictionnaire'

et l'Album qui 'seul était destiné à faire la deuxième partie de *Bouvard et Pécuchet*'. Il indique de quelle façon le dictionnaire était déjà entré dans les livres de Flaubert. Mais c'est d'un seul trait qu'il se prouve le profond flaubertien, et se distingue de tous les philologues secs. Il montre sa compréhension profonde de son héros, quand il déclare:

'...depuis le jour où petit enfant il notait déjà les bêtises d'une vieille dame qui venait en visite chez sa mère.'

Comme critique cela vaut bien tous les arguments élaborés.

Qu'est-ce que l'*Ulysses*[1] de James Joyce? Ce roman appartient à la grande classe de romans en forme de sonate, c'est-à-dire, dans la forme: thème, contre-thème, rencontre, développement, finale. Et à la subdivision: roman père-et-fils. Il suit la grande ligne de l'*Odyssée*, et présente force correspondances plus ou moins exactes avec les incidents du poème d'Homère. Nous y trouvons Télémaque, son père, les sirènes, le Cyclope, sous des travestissements inattendus, baroques, argotiques, véridiques et gigantesques.

Les romanciers n'aiment dépenser que trois mois, six mois pour un roman. Joyce y a mis quinze ans. Et *Ulysses* est plus condensé (732 grandes feuilles) que n'importe quelle œuvre entière de Flaubert; on y découvre plus d'architecture.

Il y a des pages incomparables dans *Bovary*, des paragraphes incomparablement condensés dans *Bouvard* (voir celui où on achète les sacrés-cœurs, images pieuses,

[1] Shakespeare et Cie, éditeur, 12, rue de l'Odéon, Paris.

etc.). Il y a des pages de Flaubert qui exposent leur matière aussi rapidement que les pages de Joyce, mais Joyce a complété le grand sottisier. Dans un seul chapitre il décharge tous les clichés de la langue anglaise, comme un fleuve ininterrompu. Dans un autre chapitre il enferme toute l'histoire de l'expression verbale anglaise, depuis les premiers vers allitérés (c'est le chapitre dans l'hôpital où on attend la parturition de Mrs Purefoy). Dans un autre on a les 'en-tête' du *Freeman's Journal* depuis 1760, c'est-à-dire l'histoire du journalisme; et il fait cela sans interrompre le courant de son livre.

Il s'exprime différemment dans les différentes parties de son livre (comme le permet même Aristote), mais ce n'est pas, comme le dit le distingué Larbaud, qu'il abandonne l'unité de style. Chaque personnage, non seulement parle à sa propre guise, mais il pense à sa propre guise, ce n'est pas plus abandonner l'unité de style que quand les divers personnages d'un roman dit de style uni parlent de manières diverses: on omet les guillemets, voilà tout.

Bloom, commis de publicité, l'Ulysse du roman, l'homme moyen sensuel, la base, comme le sont Bouvard et Pécuchet, de la démocratie, l'homme qui croit ce qu'il lit dans les journaux, souffre χατὰ θυμόν. Il s'intéresse à tout, veut expliquer tout pour impressionner tout le monde. Non seulement il est un 'moyen' littéraire beaucoup plus rapide, beaucoup plus apte à ramasser ce qu'on dit et pense partout, ce que les gens quelconques disent et remâchent cent fois par semaine, mais les autres personnages sont choisis pour l'aider, pour ramasser les vanités des milieux autres que le sien.

Bouvard et Pécuchet sont séparés du monde, dans

une sorte d'eau dormante. Bloom, au contraire, s'agite dans un milieu beaucoup plus contagieux.

Joyce emploie un échafaudage pris à Homère, et les restes d'une culture moyenâgeuse allégorique; peu importe, c'est une affaire de cuisine, qui ne restreint pas l'action, qui ne l'incommode pas, qui ne nuit pas à son réalisme, ni à la contemporanéité de son action. C'est un moyen de régler la forme. Le livre a plus de forme que n'en ont les livres de Flaubert.

Télémaque, Stephen, fils spirituel de Bloom, commence par réfléchir sur une vanité moyenâgeuse, ramassée dans une école catholique; il prolonge une vanité universitaire, le rapport entre Hamlet et Shakespeare. Toujours réaliste dans le plus stricte sens flaubertien, toujours documenté, documenté sur la vie même, Joyce ne dépasse jamais le moyen. Le réalisme cherche une généralisation qui agit non seulement sur le nombre, sur la multiplicité, mais dans la permanence. Joyce combine le moyen âge, les ères classiques, même l'antiquité juive, dans une action actuelle; Flaubert échelonne les époques.

Dans son élimination acharnée des guillemets, Joyce présente l'épisode du Cyclope avec les paroles ordinaires, mais à côté il pose la grandiloquence, parodie et mesure de la différence entre le réalisme et un romantisme de fanfaron. J'ai dit que la critique vraie vient des auteurs; ainsi Joyce à propos de Sainte Antoine: 'On pourrait le croire s'il (Flaubert) nous avait présenté Antoine à Alexandrie gobant les femmes et les objets de luxe.'

Un seul chapitre de *Ulysses* (157 pages) correspond à la *Tentation de saint Antoine*. Stephen, Bloom et Lynch se trouvent ivres dans un bordel; tout le grotesque de leur pensée est mis à nu; pour la première fois, depuis

Dante, on trouve les harpies, les furies, vivantes, les symboles pris dans le réel, dans l'actuel; rien ne dépend de la mythologie, ni de la foi dogmatique. Les proportions se réaffirment.

Le défaut de *Bouvard et Pécuchet*, défaut que signale même M. Descharmes, est que les incidents ne se suivent pas avec une nécessité assez impérieuse; le plan ne manque pas de logique, mais un autre aurait suffi. On peut avancer une thèse plus élogieuse pour Flaubert, mais si bref, si clair, et si condensé que soit *Bouvard et Pécuchet*, l'ensemble manque un peu d'entrain.

Joyce a remédié à cela; à chaque instant le lecteur est tenu prêt à tout, à chaque instant l'imprévu arrive; jusqu'aux tirades les plus longues et les plus cataloguées, on se tient aux aguets.

L'action se passe en un jour (732 pages), dans un seul endroit, Dublin. Télémaque erre παρὰ θῖνα πολυφλοίσβοιο θαλάσσης; il voit les sages-femmes avec leur sac professionnel. Ulysse déjeune, circule: messe, funérailles, maison de bains, tuyaux des courses; les autres personnages circulent; le savon circule; il cherche la publicité, l''ad' de la maison Keyes, il visite la bibliothèque nationale pour vérifier un détail anatomique de la mythologie, il vient à l'île d'Aeolus (bureau d'un journal), tous les bruits éclatent, tramways, camions, wagons des postes, etc.; Nausikaa se montre, on dîne à l'hôpital: rencontre d'Ulysse et de Télémaque, bordel, combat, retour chez Bloom, et puis l'auteur présente Pénélope, symbole de la terre, dont les pensées de nuit terminent le récit, balançant les ingéniosités mâles.

Cervantes ne parodiait qu'une seule folie littéraire, la

folie chevaleresque. Seuls Rabelais et Flaubert attaquent tout un siècle, s'opposent à toute une encyclopédie imbécile, — sous la forme de fiction. On ne discute pas ici les Dictionnaires de Voltaire et de Bayle. Entrer dans la classe Rabelais-Flaubert n'est pas peu de chose.

Comme pages les plus acharnées on peut citer la scène du bourreau, satire plus mordante qu'aucune autre depuis que Swift proposa un remède à la disette en Irlande : manger les enfants. Partout dans les litanies ; dans la généalogie de Bloom, dans les paraphrases d'éloquence, l'œuvre est soignée, pas une ligne, une demi-ligne qui ne reçoive une intensité intellectuelle incomparable dans un livre de si longue haleine ; ou qu'on ne sait comparer qu'aux pages de Flaubert et des Goncourt.

Cela peut donner une idée du travail énorme de ces quinze ans troublés de pauvreté, de mauvaise santé, de guerre : toute la première édition de son livre 'Dubliners' brûlée, la fuite de Trieste, une opération à l'œil ; autant de faits qui n'expliquent rien du roman, dont toute l'action se passe le 16 juin 1904 à Dublin. On peut trouver des personnages disséqués d'une page, comme dans *Bovary* (voir Father Conmee, le gosse Dignam, etc.). On peut examiner les descriptions encyclopédiques, la maison rêvée de Bloom, avec texte de bail imaginaire ; toute la bouillabaisse pseudo-intellectuelle des prolétaires se présente, toute équilibrée par Pénélope, la femme, qui ne respecte nullement cet amas de nomenclatures, vagin, symbole de la terre, mer morte dans laquelle l'intelligence mâle retombe.

C'est un roman réaliste par excellence, chaque caractère parle à sa guise, et correspond à une réalité extérieure. On présente l'Irlande sous le joug britannique, le monde sous le joug de l'usure démesurée. Descharmes demande (page 267):

'Qui donc a réussi dans cette tentative quasi surhumaine de montrer, sous forme de roman et d'œuvre d'art, le pignoufisme universel?'

J'offre la réponse: si ce n'est pas James Joyce, c'est un auteur qu'il faut encore attendre; mais la réponse de cet Irlandais mérite un examen approfondi. *Ulysses* n'est pas un livre que tout le monde va admirer, pas plus que tout le monde n'admire *Bouvard et Pécuchet*, mais c'est un livre que tout écrivain sérieux a besoin de lire, qu'il sera contraint de lire afin d'avoir une idée nette du point d'arrivée de notre art, dans notre métier d'écrivain.

Rien d'étonnant si les livres de Joyce ne furent pas accueillis en Irlande en 1908; le public rustre et les provinciaux de Dublin étaient alors en train de manifester contre les drames de Synge, les trouvant un attentat à la dignité nationale. Les mêmes drames viennent d'être représentés cette année à Paris comme propagande et comme preuve de la culture de la race irlandaise. Ibsen, si je me rappelle, n'habitait pas la Norvège: Galdos, dans *Doña Perfecta*, nous montre les dangers de posséder une culture, pas même internationale, mais seulement madrilène, dans une ville de province, que l'on devine être Saragosse. Quant aux 'ainés' romantiques en Irlande, je les crois simplement incapables de comprendre ce que c'est que le réalisme. Pour George Moore et Shaw, il est de la nature humaine de ne pas vouloir se voir éclipsé par un écrivain de plus grande importance qu'eux-mêmes. On sait qu'à Dublin on lit Joyce en cachette. Ce manque de cordialité n'a rien d'étonnant. Mais la loi américaine, sous laquelle fut supprimée quatre fois la *Little Review* pour les fragments d'*Ulysses*, est une curiosité tellement curieuse, une telle démonstration de la mentalité des légistes incultes, des spécialistes illettrés, qu'il mérite bien l'attention des psychologues européens, ou plutôt des spécialistes en méningites. Non, mes chers amis, la démocratie (qu'il faut tant sauvegarder, selon notre feu calamité Wilson) n'a rien de commun avec la liberté personnelle, ni avec la déférence fraternelle de Koung-fu-Tseu.

Section 211, du code pénal des États-Unis d'Amérique (je traduis mot à mot, dans l'ordre du texte):

'Chaque obscène, impudique, lascif, et chaque sale livre, pamphlet, tableau, papier, lettre, écriture, cliché, ou autre publication de caractère indécent et chaque article ou objet désigné, adapté ou fait dans l'intention d'empêcher la conception ou pour provoquer l'avortement ou pour tout usage indécent ou immoral et chaque article, instrument, substance, drogue, médecine ou objet auquel on donne la publicité, ou qu'on décrit d'une façon à pousser une autre personne à l'employer, ou à l'appliquer pour empêcher la conception ou pour obtenir l'avortement ou pour tout but indécent ou immoral, et chaque écrit, ou imprimé, carte-lettre, feuillet, livre, pamphlet, avertissement, ou notice de toute espèce qui donne information, directement ou indirectement de comment, ou du quel, ou par quel moyen desdits articles ou choses peuvent être obtenu ou fait, ou d'où, ou par lequel, tout acte opération de toute espèce pour obtenir ou produire l'avortement, sera fait ou exécuté, ou comment ou par lesquels moyens la conception peut être empêchée ou l'avortement produit, ou cacheté ou non cacheté, et chaque lettre, paquet, colis ou autres

objets postaux qui contiennent aucun sale, vil, indécent
objet, artifice, ou substance, chaque et tout papier,
écriture ou avis qu'aucun article, instrument, substance,
drogue, médecine ou objet puisse ou peut être employé
ou appliqué pour l'empêchement de la conception ou
pour la production de l'avortement, pour aucun but
indécent ou immoral, et chaque description destinée à
induire ou à inciter personne à employer ainsi ou
appliquer tel article, instrument, substance, drogue,
médecine, ou objet est par ceci déclaré être matière non
recevable à la poste, et ne doit pas être porté à la poste,
ni distribué par aucun bureau des postes, par aucun
facteur des postes. Quiconque déposera, à son escient,
ou fera déposer pour être transporté un objet déclaré
par cette section non recevable à la poste, ou à son escient,
prendra, ou fera prendre par la poste afin de la faire
circuler ou distribuer, ou d'aider à la dite circulation et
distribution, subira une amende de 5000 (cinq mille)
dollars au maximum ou un emprisonnement de cinq
ans, au maximum, ou les deux peines à la fois.'

C'est le vingtième siècle: paganisme, christianisme,
muflisme, pignoufisme; si aucun doute réside dans le
cerveau du lecteur, on peut l'éclairer par la décision d'un
juge américain, débitée à l'occasion de la troisième
suppression de la *Little Review*. Le grand avocat, collec-
tionneur d'art moderne, chevalier de votre Légion
d'honneur, John Quinn fit le plaidoyer pour la littérature: les classiques même, dit-il, ne peuvent échapper à
de telles imbécillités.

La voix de la Thémis états-unisienne lui répond (citation du Juge Hand):

'Je ne doute guère que beaucoup d'œuvres vraiment

grandes qui entreraient dans cette prescription, si on les soumettait aux épreuves couramment et souvent employées, échappent de temps à autre seulement parce qu'elles entrent dans la catégorie des "classiques"; il est entendu pour la mise en acte de cette loi qu'elles ont ordinairement l'immunité d'intervention parce qu'elles ont la sanction de l'antiquité et de la renommée, et font appel, ordinairement, à un nombre relativement restreint de lecteurs.'

N'est-ce pas que nous avons ici deux joyaux que le grand Flaubert aurait saisis pour son Album, et que ces citations auraient même dépassé son espérance?

Quant aux deux dernières pages de Descharmes, je les regrette un peu; je me réserve le privilège de croire que Spinoza avait la tête plus solide que M. Paul Bourget. Et si la pensée en soi est un mal nuisible à l'humanité, je remercie, tout de même, M. Descharmes pour s'en être tant donné.

MR ELIOT'S SOLID MERIT

As Confucius has remarked: It is easy to run to excesses; it is hard to stand firm in the middle. During the past 20 years the chief or average complaint against the almost reverend Eliot has been that he exaggerated his moderations. A cross-cut of three generations' opinion as received at this office since the initiation of my present series of notes on England's Helicon and Rhadamanthus seems to indicate considerable need of re-examination of our eminent confrère, not in respect to isolated discourses but in his egregious entirety.

Samples of recent comment:

Well known author in his thirties says: Oh, a charrrming person! Writes the most AWFUL rott!

Ferocious contemporary of Mr E. and myself, communicating from utmost Occident: I hear you have... administered a lambasting to that weasel...please send me copies of *N.E.W.* containing....I have a score of my own to settle....I will pay for the copies....

Elderly man of letters: Yeah! I heah thet Eliot has replaced Chesterton, etc. in the English firmament...etc.

Which reminds me of the days when the *Quarterly* with its usual whatever-it-is employed a certain Waugh to denounce Eliot's best poems as the work of a 'drunken helot', possibly hunting for something approaching a pun but at any rate showing that kind of flair and literary sensibility (à rebours) which have characterized the Albemarle Street congeries from its inception and will probably last as long as cabbage emits an odour when boiling.

If Mr Eliot weren't head and shoulders above the rank of the organized pifflers, and if he didn't amply deserve his position as recognized head of English literary criticism I would not be wasting time, typing-ribbon and postage, to discuss his limitations at all.

Our generation was brought up in absolute economic illiteracy. Only the most tortured and active among us have been driven to analyse the hell that surrounded us. Monetary infection has penetrated the inmost crannies of mind; the virus has been so subtle that men's minds (souls—call 'em souls if that concords with your religion) have been strangled before they knew it. How, indeed, can an animal be aware of its death if it is first narcoticized, if the death comes as a gradual sleepiness, then sleep, a creeping FIRST into the very organs of perception?

The 'pore' and a few of the most unruly writers have been up against hunger, or the imminent danger of hunger; been dumped on the pavement with half-a-crown for their fortune, and thereby jabbed into thinking; but the deep evil has come during sleep; we have, almost to a man, been infected when we LEAST KNEW it; when we least intended an evil.

The great division in all—I mean ALL, contemporary writing—is between that little that has been written by men who had 'clarified their intentions'; who were writing with the *sole aim* of registering and communicating truth or their desire, and the overwhelming bulk composed of the consciously dishonest *and* of those whose writing has been affected at second or tenth remove by economic pressure, economic temptation, economic flattery, by 'if you can only put it in the right form' and so on.

If I, who have always been a banned writer, have discovered this, what is to be said of the 'victors'?

There are all degrees and nuances, from the poor damn'd cringing hacks who fluff up and say they only write what they think, and that 'of course they will answer questions' and then slink off beaten and silent when you ask them anything vital, or who boast that their expression is not limited, merely, that they never WANT to run further than the end of the chain, up through the men who aren't for sale but get a little, just a little, good-natured or perhaps only humorous.

Eliot has paid the penalty of success. Given the amount of that success, the low degree of penalty paid is proof of his solid capacity.

I am not throwing eggs at a man whose writing is vastly more welcome than mine is. The reader is offered my *own case* for his anatomic study. I have always been a banned writer. Five years ago there was talk of an edition of my criticisms in about 20 volumes. It was to be 'complete', etc. I could recall no occasion on which I had written anything against my belief and conscience. But when I gathered up the mass of printed material, I found that nothing that I had been really paid for in money was of the least permanent interest. I mean, distinctly, what I had written as free agent, say for the *Little Review* was the solidest; what I had written at a guinea a shot for Orage was worth gleaning; but no article for which I had been paid three or five guineas was worth a hoot.

There were a few apparent exceptions. I mean essays for which I had been paid fifteen or ten guineas; but in each case these were compendia of material that had cost from £100 to £400 to collect. I mean that no man could have been fed during the necessary periods of research for less than that sum, and, in certain instances, there would have been expenses of travel to be added, so that one's 'sale' was at least 80 per cent or 90 per cent below cost and one's labour was as anti-economic or anti-monetary as could be imagined.

Cuts both ways? That is to say a number of Eliot's essays might never have been written if there hadn't been a skulking anonymity in the background holding out much-needed lumps of fifteen guineas. The fact that the need of guineas existed is no commendation of our verminous fiscal system. The fact that capitalist society, in its last vile chankerous phases, has set NO value whatsodamnever on fine perception or on literary capacity, is nothing in favour of that order, either as social or mental. It deserves its overlords, as they would be estimated by a biologist, a physiognomist or a specialist in obese pathology.[1]

---

[1] The most typical are the most anonymous, the least anxious for publicity. E.g. I recall the nervousness of Herb. Hoover before the cinema camera. Some faces are eloquent. The scandalous tightening of the libel laws in England is clear symptom of the cowardice of modern power, its desire to hide. Zaharoff, De Wendel and their financial affiliates avoid newspaper notice when possible. 'We are tired', said the greatest of the moderns, 'of a government in which there is NO responsible person, having a front name, a hind name and an address.'

MR ELIOT'S SOLID MERIT

The merit of an author who can pass through the dolorous gates and write *in* the 'citta dolente' among the unstill gibberings of 'fellow reviewers', 'fellow employees', doddering geezers doing notes on 60 volumes a week, etc. AND still enrich formal discussion of heterogeneous writers with paragraphs as clear, and deep, as incisive and as subtle as the delicate incision of a great surgeon, IS A POSITIVE MERIT, and it is a merit whereto Eliot almost ALONE in our time could lay any valid or sustainable claim.

After recovering from one's irritation that an intelligent man CAN, or could a decade ago, still write about Ben Jonson in language that could get into the *Times Literary Supplement*; after recovering from the quite foolish and misguided attempt to read through the *Selected Essays*, one can by using it properly, i.e. as grazing ground in unhurried (if any) hours, find critical estimates so just that one must believe them permanent part of literary valuation. They may not be of commanding immediacy, but that is all that could possibly be urged against them with any justice, and IMMEDIACY itself is of small use unless it be built up on a mass of EXACT knowledge, *almost* any detail of which might be stigmatized as 'minor'.

When I use the term 'blue china' in abuse, I should define it as 'minor detail' that is NOT being correlated for the sake either of IMMEDIACY or of justice, and in regard to which it is permitted one to suppose (on evidence offered) that the blue-chinite is void of any intention so to use it, or may even have forgotten (or been congenitally cramped with unawareness of) such possible uses.

'Even if we except also Jonson and Chapman, those two were notably erudite, and were notably men who *incorporated their erudition into their sensibility*: their mode of feeling was directly and freshly altered by their reading and thought. In Chapman especially there is a direct sensuous apprehension of thought, or a recreation of thought into feeling....'

'Two most powerful poets of the century....Each of these men performed certain poetic functions so magnificently well that the magnitude of the effect concealed the absence of others.'

'A philosophical theory which has entered into poetry is established, for its truth or *falsity in one* sense ceases to matter, and its truth in *another* sense is proved.'

'Interesting to speculate whether it is not a misfortune that two of the greatest masters of diction in our language, Milton and Dryden, triumph with a dazzling disregard of the soul.'

'Sometimes tell us to "look into our hearts and write". But that is not looking deep enough; Racine or Donne looked into a good deal more than the heart. One must look into the cerebral cortex, the nervous system, and the digestive tracts.'

The first and second of these quotations (italics mine) are certainly NOT dead academicism, pedantry or mere university lecturing. They are criticism definitely shot at NEW creation; at a reinvigoration of writing.

If the 3rd, 4th and 5th excite discussion it is fundamental discussion; it is not aimed at producing a quiet reposing place for anonymities (as, for example, the editor X. R.), who slouch crumbling and cringing on the margin of the literature that provides them with beef and board; who have never signed a statement or answered a question in their 20 or 40 years of trading, maggots living in or on the mental activity of their time but contributing nothing to its life, parasites in the strict sense, with the mind one would suppose inherent in parasitic condition.

That any man should have been able to get past such obstacle and to print paragraphs of literary criticism that will last as long as there are any students of English poetry concerned with just opinion and assessment of its value, is not only reason for tribute and compliment, but is an inalienable certificate of the native and persistent vigour and acuteness of an author's perceptions.

Economically Mr Eliot is perfectly justified in deriving sustenance from English or American milieux and institutions which normally give little or no welcome to literary perception. One can but rejoice that their inherited stuffiness should have been at least to some degree subjected to ventilation.

All of which is no reason to sit round rubbing one's hands, or pretending that he has triumphantly finished the job of infusing life into Universities whose rulers do NOT want it. Short of murdering a few dozen American college presidents, beginning with Nic. Butler, or patiently waiting for all his generation to die, I see almost no modus of accomplishing this desired result in America. Naturally such activism as that implied in the first alternative is alien to Mr Eliot's sensibilities, contrary to English and American Common Law (if not in the law's intention, at least in minor technical aspects) and therefore cannot be seriously considered even by an author like myself who might otherwise take considerable pleasure in transit by the shortest possible road.

All we can do is to suggest an increasing disesteem of saboteurs of the intellect, coupled with, say, daily and vigorous expression of it (the said disesteem).

As Mr Eliot is a younger man than I am, I see no reason why he should lie down on his achievements, or why cantankerous observers should despair of his further utility.

'ABJECT AND UTTER FARCE'[1]

If any reader think that this essay is not the specific concern of teachers and students of English, and if any teacher think I am dragging in extraneous matter, let him or her consider the difference between the IDEOGRAMIC method and the medieval or 'logical' method.

The so-called 'logical' method permitted the methodist to proceed from inadequate cognizance to a specious and useless conclusion; these methodists then took great pleasure in thinking that they had moved in a straight instead of a crooked line between these unfortunate states.

This is *not* good enough for the age of Marconi. Paul de Kruif's heroes, his fighters against hunger and microbes, gather their evidence, heap up their facts, often heteroclitic, and their contemporaries in any humane exercise of intellectual honesty are required to pursue analogous labours. The ideogramic method in the study of literature attained consciousness in Ernest Fenollosa. The intellectual squalor of his and of my generation made it for a long time almost impossible to get his reflections printed.

The scientist to-day heaps together his facts and has to find organizations that fit them. He must consider his field of reference. Here the philological methods fall

[1] *Harkness Hoot*, Nov. 1933.

all to pieces. American universities took over a decomposed system from the Germans. German education, especially higher education, had become a tool of Wilhelmstrasse; there is no use going into the past history of its perversion. It had become a mass means of *deflecting* the scholar's attention from the field of reference, and getting him ever further and further down his mouse hole.

Set aside such scientific training as had a very clear and specific objective, to cure some disease, to plug a particular tooth, to run up steel girders so they would stay up for a given time. What did education in literature, sociology, philosophy of our time amount to; and what spirit governed these branches? What was our field of reference? Was it ever referred to in the class-room?

Chuck the past and come to the present. The teachers of English are custodians of the means of communication IN the American social ord- or disord-er.[1]

The present accounting system murdered five million men between 1914 and 1918. It has done its utmost to suppress all the arts. It has maintained slums and poverty for twenty years when there was absolutely NO need for the continuance of these infamies. What are the teachers to DO about it?

Academic superstition is best expressed in the words of one of America's 'leading economists': 'Nothing can be done about it until....'

Every professor in America would have given the

---

[1] Mr Eliot at this point exhorts me to bring it home that this disease is not local; that England better be warned not only by America but by herself. In fact he goes so far as to say: 'What the blighters wont see is...that it is one system and a Bad one.'

same answer, or varied it with: 'Nothing can be done about it *now*.'

Julian Benda, some years ago, wrote a dull book with a good title: *La Trahison des Clercs*, using '*clerc*' in the old sense, meaning the *treason of the educated*.

And the enormity of this treason is so overwhelming that one doesn't know which corner of it to begin on. It is like a collapsed circus-tent over our heads.

For example, the Carnegie Peace Endowment costs the American public half a million a year. The founder's intention was perfectly clear. All the work that organization is paid to do has been done OUTSIDE it, either by private individuals or by the specifically British 'Union of Democratic Control'.

The proofs that scattered individuals have sought for the past fifteen or thirty years are now available in a dozen volumes, such as: *Mercanti di Cannoni*;[1] Brockway's *Bloody Traffic*; *Life of Zaharoff*; *Secret International*; *Le Crapouillot*; *L'Abominable Venalité de la Presse*.

Years ago, we 'knew' in a general way; but it has taken time to dig out the indisputable details. We know now that all the war powers helped their enemies continue the war, that every nation used material, gun sights, fuses, etc., produced by the enemies, and that this traffic went on through the war; that men were sent out in defective airplanes in order that individuals should make slightly larger profits, etc. We know that the war-causes were in great part economic.

[1] E.g. *I Mercanti di Cannoni*. Anonymous ('per evitare all' Autore le rappresaglie dei mercanti di cannoni'), Milan, 1932. Edizioni Corbaccio, Lire 10. Thus in 1933. In 1934 the list of these books is much longer.

And to this knowledge the paid bureaucracy of the Carnegie Endowment has contributed nothing whatever. If any man is more responsible for this defection than Nicholas Butler, it would be interesting to know who. If there had been one educated man of strong personality anywhere in the organization, he could have saved humanity fifteen years' time.

Count Mensdorf, the head of the Austrian section, did on at least one occasion point out that the causes of war were a *suitable* subject of study, and sent a brief list of indisputable causes to the central American office.... That office is, like every other office, a bureaucracy.

Does it matter?

I am not attacking any one man. I point out that these things result from a state of mind, and that for every criminal, there are three dozen tolerators. The psychology of the college graduate of my generation bade him hunt for a comfortable corner 'inside the system'. It was the decadence of Sam Smiles' philosophy.

Witness my post-bag for this week: A famous novelist writes me that he has been very clever, and by foreseeing the general calamity had got enough from slick deals to pay for his season abroad; he says the thing is to 'get yours, inside the system'.

The whole of my college generation was brought up to look for a job. It was admitted that there weren't nearly enough jobs, and Doc. Shelling also pointed out that, after producing an instrument (i.e. a philologist) of the utmost refinement, that instrument would be put to doing the grossest possible work.

A graduate student writes me from the American West: 'Acceptance of your programme (which is the only one of any value) would entail reform of whole methods of teaching literature, and there are too many professors who are anxious to keep their jobs, to approve of your programme.'

A young Englishman writes from Oxford: 'Never until I got here did I realize, etc. . . . the justness of your attack on the academies in *How to Read*.'[1]

Years ago, I remonstrated with a millionaire provost about the curriculum and methods in his pet university; he replied: 'I know nothing about all that. I wanted to leave a monument to my father.'

A few years later, when I wanted to get a fellowship for a writer who then needed the money, and whose name is now a household word in America, the head of an English Department proclaimed to me that: 'The University is not here for the unusual man.'

I. What does this mean? It means putrid thinking; it means short-sightedness in an extreme degree. That professor was too stupid to understand that unless the teaching interests the best mind in the class, the class goes to sleep from the top. If the best mind, or the best pair or trio of minds, in ANY class is kept awake, the enthusiasm will spread through the whole class, or, at least, to as much of the class as is ever going to take any interest in the given subject or *do* anything about it.

The gross idiocy in teaching cultural subjects, in comparison with the intelligence which has brought about the advance in material sciences, can be no more glaringly shown than in this fumble on the part of a

[1] *How to Read*, by Ezra Pound (Desmond Harmsworth, 1931). Reprinted, I think, by TO Publishers, Brooklyn and Le Beausset (Var.), 1932 (?).

highly (by some people) esteemed Head of English in one of our largest universities. And the chap isn't a bad writer of essays either. He is no worse an idiot than three dozen other elderly gents tucked into comfortable semi-sinecures.

II. The putridity of University Education, as I knew it, arose from:

(A) Total lack of direction;
(B) Utter defect in considering the field of reference.

That field was:

I. Society in general;
II. The general intellectual life of the country.

And the economic factor does enter; teachers and farmers have been for ages, and notoriously, the worst paid members of the community. Dean Saunders of Hamilton once spoke to me of 'That fine old word "an independence"', meaning sufficient income to live on, so that a man could do what he liked.

Outside the training of teachers of economics, I never in my undergraduate days heard of the subject. One was not encouraged to think about 'such things'. There was no general talk or general interest in it, or in any other general subject among members of the student body. Occasionally, there would be a vague rumour of scandal, as when Scott Nearing got fired. One didn't exactly know why; he had been thinking and talking.

No professor was, or is, expected to know anything he wasn't TAUGHT as a student.

I do not regret having taken no interest in these subjects from 1901 to 1905; there was nothing being taught then about economics that was very much worth learning. There was very little in the curricula that concerns life in the 1930's.

What there could have been, and should have been, was a little intellectual curiosity. This can exist among very ignorant men. It is probably very rare among half-educated men looking for jobs, or hoping to 'stay in' their jobs.

'I ACCUSE', 'IT IS ONLY HUMAN', etc.

Where does this bring us?

The titular head of American intellectual life is, one might suppose, the president of the American Academy. The Paris Edition of the *Chicago Tribune* recently declined to print a list of members of this 'Academy' on the grounds that such publication would be 'libellous'. The president of that academy is typical of the era that endured Harding, Coolidge, and Hoover; that eagerly bought a five cent paper telling 'em Kreuger was 'more than a financial titan', and so forth.

The whole American University situation is overcrowded by job-holders. The decent chaps from whom, in my student days, I learned particular things (about languages, for example) were men without any power whatsoever. They were timorous and resigned. They were 'safe'; they had their jobs, not very well paid, but still jobs. They could be let alone to read in their studies, disturbed only by the necessity of getting to class-room now and again. They hadn't any power. They couldn't even get printed, many of them were too modest greatly to want to. They were contemporaries of Remy de Gourmont, and they were probably wise in their generation. There probably wasn't then anything to *do* about it.

Also in my fortnight's correspondence is a letter from a man high up in a press syndicate: 'Of course the Revolution has taken place; but the press hasn't been *told* yet.' There you have it; there is NO contemporary newspaper in America.

And at the other end of the world of print or educational utterance, you have the head of an Academy whom I personally regard as a black scoundrel, a criminal. In any other trust, in any material business, he could be 'had up'. If an endowment were 'entrusted' to a living public conscience instead of tucked away in charge of 'trustees', a group of men getting half a million a year for NOT DOING what they are paid for, could be dealt with rather severely.

I don't accuse the economists of America, and the American professors, of stupidity alone, or of not being open to new ideas. I accuse them of abject lack of knowledge and of abject deficiency of curiosity. Whether in literature or in economics, they ignore and, in most cases, are IGNORANT OF simple historical facts dating from 1600, dating from 1860, dating from 1830, dating from the time of Ghengis or Pisistratus or whenever you like.

The utter bunk offered by men in power, by 'experts and authorities', could only be offered to a grossly ignorant public, and a grossly timorous intelligentsia.

Whether it be in refusal to compare one literature with another, or to bring out significant historic facts, the love of retaining a job with a salary predominates over all intellectual hunger.

The best information at my disposal indicates that research into increased efficiency of co-ordinated machinery was done almost secretly at Columbia. Dexter Kimball prints a mass of significant fact, but refrains from drawing conclusions.

The first moderately clean national administration we have had in twenty years offers suggestions that would be howled down by any public that had ever heard of the Monte dei Paschi (a bank founded in Siena in 1624). The public doesn't even know that France has had an auxiliary currency since 1919, issued not by the national government, but by the correlated and united chambers of commerce.

It is all of a piece and paste. At the age of forty-eight I am just learning things that I could perfectly well have been told at eighteen, and that, with a decent educational system, I *would* have been told at eighteen.

I swear that in all my career I have had FOUR useful hints from my living literary predecessors: one from Yeats, one from Madox Ford, one from Bridges, and one, possibly the best, from Thomas Hardy. That is to say, I have passed twenty-five years of my life in the highest possible literary company; I have known the top-notchers, and 'nigh on to fifty years of age', by means of continuous practice, and after having written the music of two operas in order to get the best work of Villon and Cavalcanti out of prisoning print and into three-dimensional sonority, I am just finding out simple fundamentals. And by heaven, my predecessors and contemporaries have lived in a state of ignorance and indifference that is almost incredible.

A REFORM NEEDS:

(1) More respect for text-books; I mean for the text-book as a composition in itself. Gaston Paris and

Solomon Reinach didn't think it beneath their dignity to write text-books; France profited by their good sense. When the distribution of text-books sinks to being a mere racket, public intelligence suffers.

(II) The IDEOGRAMIC METHOD must be applied in the making of text-books *all along the line*.

The worst howlers in the *English Journal*[1] are due, not to stupidity or incapacity to think, but to neglect of confrontations between facts relevant to the subjects discussed.

Twenty-five factors in a given case may have NO LOGICAL connection the one with any other. Cf.: A definition of fever which excluded typhoid would be unscientific. Knowledge cannot be limited to a collection of definitions.

Human nature? Yes, very human for any man to be irritated by the presentation of ANY fact whatsoever that upsets his preconceived notions. But until education welcomes any and every fact, it will remain what it now is, a farce.

Sales resistance is nothing in comparison with fact resistance and idea-resistance.

In response to a request to lengthen the foregoing exhortation I offer its sequel. The *English Journal* having declined the foregoing pages, I think on grounds of decorum, they were, eleven months later, induced to put forth something which their editor considered more suitable to his disciples.

---

[1] The *English Journal* is the bulletin of teachers of English in the American school system.

THE TEACHER'S MISSION[1]

I

'Artists are the antennae of the race.' If this statement is incomprehensible and if its corollaries need any explanation, let me put it that a nation's writers are the voltometers and steam-gauges of that nation's intellectual life. They are the registering instruments, and if they falsify their reports there is no measure to the harm that they do. If you saw a man selling defective thermometers to a hospital, you would consider him a particularly vile kind of cheat. But for 50 years an analogous treatment of thought has gone on in America without throwing any discredit whatever on its practitioners.

For this reason I personally would not feel myself guilty of manslaughter if by any miracle I ever had the pleasure of killing Canby or the editor of the *Atlantic Monthly* and their replicas, or of ordering a wholesale death and/or deportation of a great number of affable, suave, moderate men, all of them perfectly and smugly convinced of their respectability, and all incapable of any twinge of conscience on account of any form of mental cowardice or any falsification of reports whatsoever.

Criminals have no intellectual interests. Is it clear to the teacher of literature that writers who falsify their registration, sin against the well-being of the nation's

[1] *English Journal*, 1934.

mind? Is there any possible 'voice from the audience' that can be raised to sustain the contrary? Is there any reader so humble of mind as to profess incomprehension of this statement?

In so far as education and the press have NOT blazoned this view during our time, the first step of educational reform is to proclaim the necessity of HONEST REGIS-TRATION, and to exercise an antiseptic intolerance of all inaccurate reports about letters—intolerance of the same sort that one would exercise about a false hospital chart or a false analysis in a hospital laboratory.

This means abolition of personal vanity in the re-porting; it means abolition of this vanity whether the writer is reporting on society at large; on the social and economic order, or on literature itself. It means the abolition of local vanity. You would not tolerate a doctor who tried to tell you the fever temperature of patients in Chicago was always lower than that of sufferers from the same kind of fever in Singapore (unless accurate instruments registered such a differ-ence).

As the press, daily, weekly, and monthly, is utterly corrupted, either from economic or personal causes, it is manifestly UP TO the teaching profession to act for themselves without waiting for the journalists and magazine blokes to assist them.

The mental life of a nation is no one man's private property. The function of the teaching profession is to maintain the HEALTH OF THE NATIONAL MIND. As there are great specialists and medical discoverers, so there are 'leading writers'; but once a discovery is made, the local practitioner is just as inexcusable as the discoverer himself if he fails to make use of known remedies and known prophylactics.

A vicious economic system has corrupted every ramification of thought. There is no possibility of ultimately avoiding perception of this. The first act is to recognize the disease, the second to cure it.

II

The shortcomings of education and of the professor are best tackled by each man for himself; his first act must be an examination of his consciousness, and his second, the direction of his will toward the light.

The first symptom he finds will, in all probability, be mental LAZINESS, lack of curiosity, desire to be undisturbed. This is not in the least incompatible with the habit of being very BUSY along habitual lines.

Until the teacher wants to know all the facts, and to sort out the roots from the branches, the branches from the twigs, and to grasp the MAIN STRUCTURE of his subject, and the relative weights and importances of its parts, he is just a lump of the dead clay in the system.

The disease of the last century and a half has been 'abstraction'. This has spread like tuberculosis.

Take the glaring example of 'Liberty'. Liberty became a goddess in the eighteenth century, and had a FORM. That is to say, Liberty was 'defined' in the *Rights of Man* as 'the right to do anything that doesn't hurt someone else'. The restricting and highly ethical limiting clause was, within a few decades, REMOVED. The idea of liberty degenerated into meaning mere irresponsibility and the right to be just as pifflingly idiotic as the laziest sub-human pleased, and to exercise almost 'any and every' activity utterly regardless of its effect on the commonweal.

I take a non-literary example, on purpose. Observing the same mental defection in literary criticism or in proclaimed programmes, we stigmatize writing which consists of 'general terms'. These general terms finally have NO meaning, in the sense that each teacher uses them with a meaning so vague as to *convey* nothing to his students.

All of which is inexcusable AFTER the era of 'Agassiz and the fish'—by which I mean now that general education is in position to profit by the parallels of biological study based on EXAMINATION and COMPARISON of particular specimens.

All teaching of literature should be performed by the presentation and juxtaposition of specimens of writing and NOT by discussion of some other discusser's opinion *about* the general standing of a poet or author. Any teacher of biology would tell you that knowledge can NOT be transmitted by general statement without knowledge of particulars. By this method of presentation and juxtaposition even a moderately ignorant teacher can transmit most of what he knows WITHOUT filling the student's mind with a great mass of prejudice and error. The teaching may be incomplete but it will not be idiotic or vicious. Ridiculous prejudice in favour of known authors, or in favour of modern as against ancient, or ancient against modern work, would of necessity disappear.

The whole system of intercommunication via the printed page in America is now, and has been, a mere matter of successive *dilutions* of knowledge. When some European got tired of an idea he wrote it down, it was printed after an interval, and it was reviewed in, say, London, by a hurried and harassed reviewer, usually lazy, almost always indifferent. The London periodicals were rediluted by still more hurried and usually incompetent New York reviewers, and their 'opinion' was dispersed and watered down via American trade distribution. Hence the 15 to 20 years' delay with which all and every idea, and every new kind of literature, reaches the 'American reader' or 'teacher'.

The average reader under such a system has no means whatsoever of controlling the facts. He has been brought up on vague general statements, which have naturally blunted his curiosity. The simple ignorance displayed, even in the *English Journal*, is appalling, and the individuals cannot always be blamed.

A calm examination of the files of the *Little Review* for 1917–19 will show the time-lag between publication and reception of perfectly simple facts. The Douglas economics now being broadcast by Senator Cutting, and receiving 'thoughtful attention from the Administration', were available in 1919, and mentionable in little magazines in America in 1920. Many people think they would have saved us from the crisis, and would have already abolished poverty, had they received adequate attention and open discussion, and started toward being put into effect at that time. I mention this to show that the time-lag in American publishing and teaching is NOT CONFINED to what are called 'merely cultural subjects' but that it affects even matters of life and death, eating or starvation, the comfort and suffering of great masses of the people.

III

Our editor asks: What ought to be done?

1. Examination of conscience and consciousness, by each teacher for himself or herself.

2. Direction of the will toward the light, with concurrent sloughing off of laziness and prejudice.

3. An inexorable demand for the facts.

4. Dispassionate examination of the ideogramic method (the examination and juxtaposition of particular specimens—e.g., particular works, passages of literature) as an implement for acquisition and transmission of knowledge.

5. A definite campaign against human deadwood still clogging the system. A demand either that the sabotage cease, or that the saboteurs be removed.

As concomitant and result, there would naturally be a guarantee that the dismissal of professors and teachers *for having* EXAMINED facts and having discussed ideas, should cease. Such suppression of the searchers for Truth is NOT suited to the era of the New Deal, and should be posted on the pillar of infamy as a symptom of the Wilson-Harding-Coolidge-Hoover epoch. To remove any teacher or professor for his IDEAS, it should be necessary to prove that these ideas had been preached from malice and against the mental health of the nation. As in our LAW a man is assumed innocent until the contrary is proved, so a man must be assumed to be of good-will until the contrary is proved.

A man of good-will abandons a false idea as soon as he is made aware of its falsity, he abandons a mis-statement of fact as soon as corrected. In the case of a teacher misinforming his students, it is the business of his higher officers to INSTRUCT him, not merely to suppress him. In the case of professors, etc., the matter should be carried in open debate.

When the University of Paris was alive (let us say in the time of Abelard) even highly technical special debates were a public exhilaration. Education that does not bear on LIFE and on the most vital and immediate problems of the day is not education but merely suffocation and sabotage.

Retrospect is inexcusable, especially in education, save when used distinctly AS a leverage toward the future. An education that is not focused on the life of to-day and to-morrow is treason to the pupil. There are no words permitted in a polite educational bulletin that can describe the dastardliness of the American university system as we have known it. By which I don't mean that the surface hasn't been, often, charming. I mean that the *fundamental* perversion has been damnable. It has tended to unfit the student for his part in his era. Some college presidents have been chosen rather for their sycophantic talents than for their intellectual acumen or their desire to enliven and build intellectual life. Others with good intentions have seen their aims thwarted and their best intended plans side-tracked, and have been compelled to teeter between high aim and constriction. The evil, like all evil, is in the direction of the will. For that phrase to have life, there must be both will *and* direction.

There may have been an excuse, or may have been extenuating circumstances for my generation, but there can be no *further* excuse. When I was in prep school Ibsen was a joke in the comics, and the great authors of the weekly 'literary' press and the 'better magazines' were . . . a set of names that are now known only to 'students of that period', and to researchers. Then came the Huneker-Brentano sabotage. New York's advanced set abandoned the Civil War, and stopped at the London nineties or the mid-European sixties and eighties. That is, the London nineties were maintained in New York up to 1915. Anything else was considered as bumptious silliness. The *Atlantic Monthly's* view of French literature in 1914 was as comic as Huey Long's opinion of Aquinas. And the pretenders, the men who then set themselves up as critics and editors, still prosper, and still prevent contemporary ideas from penetrating the Carnegie library system or from reaching the teaching profession, until they have gathered a decade's mildew—or two decades' mildew.

The humblest teacher in grammar school CAN CONTRIBUTE to the national education if he or she refuses to let printed inaccuracy pass unreproved:

(A) By acquiring even a little accurate knowledge based on examination and comparison of PARTICULAR books.

(B) By correcting his or her own errors gladly and as a matter of course, at the earliest possible moment.

For example, a well-known anthology by a widely accepted anthologist contains a mass of simple inaccuracies, statements contrary to simple, ascertainable chronology. I have not seen any complaints. In the *English Journal* inaccuracies of fact occur that ought to be corrected NOT by established authors but by junior members of the teaching profession. This would lead inevitably to a higher intellectual morale. Some teachers would LIKE it, others would have to accept it because they would not be able to continue without it. False witness in teaching of letters OUGHT to be just as dishonourable as falsification in medicine.

A LETTER FROM DR ROUSE
TO E. P.

We have computed the cost of war in its toll of young life, but its power to damage letters has not yet been weighed. Perhaps because no one has yet thought of it in relation to men who had just reached maturity in 1914.

About 50, the serious writer or composer begins to get top side of his technique and to come to grips with his subject. What happens if the bank buzzards choose that moment to let loose Armageddon?

This occurs to me, first because in the last year a whole new line of 'men now over seventy' has rather suddenly come into my world! Dr Whittaker's edition of William Young's music, knocking the text-books galley-west; Laurence Binyon's break away from the Museum, and his translation of Dante. And now the editor who has given me more pleasure than any man living, the man who made Golding's *Ovid* available, comes out of the silence with an *Odysseus* that I can read, and that all my entourage, bored for years by hearing me talk of a poem in a language they can't understand, are now engaged in reading one after another so that I couldn't get hold of the book to review it, even if such were my intention.

W. H. D. Rouse went to the right place for his

Homer—namely, to the Ægean in a sail boat, where they are still telling the same yarns even if they tell them about the prophet Elias. Dr Rouse has at last translated 'polumetis'. Salel in 1543 found a living phrase when he called Ulysses 'ce rusé personnage'; Rouse begins:

'This is the story of a man, of one who was never at a loss.' A rendering truer even than Salel's. The Doctor has told Homer to more boys than any man living. I hope he will now tell us the whole story.

Let him speak for himself. The letter was private, but we have permission to use it.

'...However I do see what wealth is: Wealth is simply food plus the luxuries of clothes and a roof, and it is the obvious duty of statesmen to provide food for the nation. Let every man grow what he can, and let the nation feed itself, and it is rich. We in England could grow 75 per cent, there is no doubt, and probably more, and the corollary would be a healthy, manly population who felt like kings, such as yeomen were. It is quite possible, for the stock is not deteriorated at all. Even the miserable doctrines of "classes" which amount simply to I grab what you've got, would go, for they depend solely on the herding of men into strata instead of grouping them in microcosms; we never thought about "class" when I was a boy...your printed questions? I don't know and I only know the politicians begin at the wrong end.

'As regards Greek, which is not wealth but food for the soul...a necessity of civilised life, we come back to *Ulysses*. I should very much like to see your criticisms. You won't offend me if you dislike anything. I hope you have the mythology by this time, composed for the like audience. One little boy sidled up to me long after in a country lane: "Sir, you know those stories you tell us? Are they true?..." But I was more pleased with another boy. The head-mistress asked him what story I had been telling last, when we were doing the *Iliad*. "Story?" he said, "He isn't telling us *stories*. He is telling us *things*."[1]

'This was when we were doing the *Iliad*, which I feared might be too psychological for them; but not a bit of it. Next term I am going to tell *Ulysses* to the village boys here at the school, age 12 plus, who know no language but English and have no books at home to speak of.

'Your remarks on the Greek Literature book, which you sent me, are very much to the point.[2] How dull are these summaries of the subject matter! And there is a whole series of books pretending to make classics easier, e.g., 20 lines of *Æneid*, half a page of gas, 30 lines, more gas, and the resultant effect a complete babel. You have no time to get into the Latin mood, and you

[1] For sidelight I offer the following anecdote from Frobenius: The blacks were being taught Æsop, as it was supposed to be a suitable text. They were still in that state where legend is living. They were not reduced to tales of the past. Their loga-laga, or whatever the term is, concerned what was going on in the present. Koja over the evening fire told his listeners what the Antelope was doing *at that moment*, what the Antelope was *saying at that moment* to the young Antelope.

The bright professorial seeker asked a black which loga-laga he preferred—his own or the white man's? Eh? Black didn't know the white had any loga-laga. But yes, the stories of Æsop. Black didn't call that loga-laga, he called that 'just copy book exercise'.

[2] (*Note.*—'Dust upon Hellas', *Time and Tide*, Nov. 10.)

are forever switching off one on to the other, just like a construing lesson.'

In an earlier letter on natural speech in translation of the classics, Dr Rouse had written:

'The characters of Homer speak naturally, very unlike "Leaf and Lang", but it happens that I have been telling the stories to little boys of 10–11 years, *with whom the frills and affectations of translators do not go down at all.*

'They are sensitive to anything really good, even if they do not understand it at all, any good sound or tone of words. The story makes clear the general sense, of course, but natural it must be.

'I found through many years the most useful critics in the world to be intelligent boys, and I told these boys of ten the whole of Homer, and all the chief Greek mythology, stories of history, and the Golden Ass. The language I used is that which I used naturally, and I learnt it from my parents and their friends, and from peasants who still use it, only leaving out the grammatical oddities of the last, which are always local.

'For boys of ten, you must make the meaning clear, if you don't their faces show it in an instant....'

RETROSPECT: INTERLUDE

A polite (by definition) essay to refute (it is impolite to refute)
tentatively; to confirm; or to leave suspended the statement of
an eminent confrère: 'Not so much came out of those hopeful, in
Paris, years.'

What should have come *out* of them? Couldn't
there have been just something *there*? Isn't
the essayist (when polite) subject almost to
the novelist's duty, and shouldn't his politeness consist
simply in affirmation of what was 'There'—in this case
in the Paris of 'those years'? a stasis, an ambience? Not
merely an elongated hen producing an abortive chicken
for the use of a half raw utterly incult 'next' generation.

Moved to bile by collected pretentious wash-lists (or
a list of soiled clothes in particular), I am called back to
an evening when Wörmser was reading something
forgotten, so far as the subject went, but unforgetable
as to the tone.

There was in those days still a Parisian research for
technique. Spire wrangled as if *vers libre* were a political
doctrine. De Souza had what the old Abbé called *une
oreille très fine*, but he, the Abbé, wrapped up De Souza's
poems and asked me to do likewise in returning them
lest his *servante* should see what I was carrying.

The Abbé was M. Rousselot who had made a machine
for measuring the duration of verbal components.
A quill or tube held in the nostril, a less shaved quill or

other tube in the mouth, and your consonants signed as you spoke them.

They return, One and by one, With fear, As half awakened each letter with a double registration of quavering. And George Fourest declaimed his account of the curious princess; which ends 'et les hermaphrodites dans les bocaux'.

All of which was 'mœurs contemporaines', Doyen keeping something together, Haulte Chambre, Jean Cassou. Doyen when I last saw him, proclaiming that Mr Hemingway's *Bolitho* was a genius. And there was that old fellow who wrote *Autour de Bouvard et Pécuchet* which I wish I could find again in my book case. There was a strata of Paris which mere criticism of books fails to get hold of, a strata that goes either into literature itself, I mean as its subject, or remains unrecorded. It is the tone of the time. It don't plop down a turtle's egg. It just stays there or drifts there. You can't pack it and ship it to Manchester.

There was, a bit later, so far as it came to the undersigned, the more glittering Paris, now everyman's Paris. Picabia gone to hell, Brancusi universally recognized by cognoscenti, Cocteau in *Vogue*, and finally Leger's photo in *Vanity Fair*. Max Ernst's BLUE faces me from the other side of this cubicle.

Ut delectet. Some demarcation between the literature that is worth setting in the GREAT record, and the ambience wherein the non-disruptive perceptions exist. The latter you record in a series of thirty novels, and the former perhaps on the back of an envelope.

I can still hear Jean de Gourmont: 'Et vous aurez fini ce soir?' Which registered the amical shock of two currents. The older civilization unresenting a difference of tempo. There was no reason for NOT starting at once to deal with *Poudre aux Moineaux*, Remy's last very brief jottings. La Marquise de Pierre gave me to understand that she had never before met an American. So that if my first little job in London had been to assure Elkin Mathews that Wm Michael Rossetti's version of the *Convito* ought to be printed, my later perambulations in Paris took me equally into a hinterland, into quite Jamesean shadows. I had seen a garden party in the Temple, in London that was 'perfect Mrs Ward', and I suppose Mr Eliot's readers have never heard of that lady. I haven't for fifteen years.

I am setting down these apparently aimless phrases so that the reader may have some sort of background, something less detailed than Umbrian clarity, some sort of retrospect, cloudy in itself, but from which the teeth and gnashings of the present, the mental incisions, can emerge and whereby they may have a chance of keeping some sort of proportion.

When I try to continue the great Henry's labours, if not to explain one race to another, at least to give them some sort of tip or of inkling as to why they do not immediately grasp the significance of following events and explosions, I come to a vision of the armistice. A very tired, mild, white haired ambassador. That must have been 1919, and I set this against my father's more vivid impression of that diplomat, a young man rushing back into a wooden 'office' (a law office) and emerging thence with a gun (that is a revolver, now a 'rod') with the avowed intention of dealing with 'that son of . . . . .' in what had been up to that moment a legal proceeding, a land office case. In Hailey, in Idaho, in or about 1885. Will Rogers' 'Judge' has reminded me that men of my time as small boys were accustomed to see just such veterans of the War of Secession as are there shown on the celluloid. We all remember freed slaves, that is to say old mammies who had been chattels.

6 December 1935

3

PREFATIO AUT CIMICIUM
TUMULUS[1]

I

M r F. V. Morley, with a misplaced sense of humour, has suggested that I write a fifty page preface to two hundred pages of contemporary poesy. This to me, who have for a quarter of a century contended that critics should know more and write less. No two hundred pages of contemporary poetry would sustain the demands I could make in half such a preface. I am moreover confining my selection to poems Britain has not accepted and in the main that the British literary bureaucracy does N O T want to have printed in England.

I shall therefore write a preface mainly about something else.

Mr Eliot and I are in agreement, or 'belong to the same school of critics', in so far as we both believe that existing works form a complete order which is changed by the introduction of the 'really new' work.

His contempt for his readers has always been much greater than mine, by which I would indicate that I quite often write as if I expected my reader to use his intelligence, and count on its being fairly strong, whereas Mr Eliot after enduring decennial fogs in Britain prac-

[1] From *Active Anthology* (1933).

tically always writes as if for very very feeble and brittle mentalities, from whom he can expect neither resilience nor any faculty for seeing the main import instead of the details or surfaces.

When he talks of 'commentation and elucidation' and of the 'correction of taste', I go into opposition, or rather, having been there first, I note that if I was in any sense the revolution I have been followed by the counter-revolution. Damn your taste, I would like if possible to sharpen your perceptions, after which your taste can take care of itself.

'Commentation' be damned. 'Elucidation' can stand if it means 'turn a searchlight on' something or preferably some work or author lying in shadow.

2

Mr Eliot's flattering obeisance to 'exponents of criticism', wherein he says that he supposes they have not assumed that criticism is an 'autotelic activity', seems to me so much apple-sauce. In so far as the bureaucracy of letters has considered their writing as anything more than a short cut to the feeding trough or a means of puffing up their personal importances, they have done little else for the past thirty years than boost the production of writing about writing, not only as autotelic, but as something which ought to receive more attention from the reading victim than the great books themselves.

Granted that nobody ought to be such a presumptuous imbecile as to hold up the autotelic false horizon, Mr Eliot describes a terrestrial paradise and not the de facto world, in which more immediate locus we observe a perpetual exchange of civilities between pulex, cimex, vermiformis, etc., each holding up his candle before the shrines of his similars.

A process having no conceivable final limit and illustratable by my present activity: I mean on this very page, engaging your attention while I talk about Mr Eliot's essay about other essayists' essays. In the course of his eminently professorial volume he must have mentioned at least forty-five essayists whom to-morrow's readers will be most happy not to hear mentioned, but mention of whom must have contributed enormously to Mr Eliot's rise to his deserved position as arbiter of British opinion.

KRINO

'Existing monuments form an ideal order among themselves.' It would be healthier to use a zoological term rather than the word monument. It is much easier to think of the *Odyssey* or *Le Testament* or Catullus' *Epithalamium* as something living than as a series of cenotaphs. After all, Homer, Villon, Propertius, speak of the world as I know it, whereas Mr Tennyson and Dr Bridges did not. Even Dante and Guido with their so highly specialized culture speak of a part of life as I know it. ATHANATOS.

However, accepting for the moment Mr Eliot's monumental or architectural simile: the KRINO, 'to pick out for oneself, choose, prefer' (page 381 my edition of Liddell and Scott) which seems to me the major job, is to determine, first, the main form and main proportions of that order of extant letters, to locate, first the greater pyramids and then, possibly, and with a decently proportioned emphasis, to consider the exact measurements of the stone-courses, layers, etc.

Dryden gives T. S. E. a good club wherewith to smack Milton. But with a modicum of familiarity or even a passing acquaintance with Dante, the club would hardly be needed.

A volume of quite sound statistical essays on poesy may quite easily drive a man to the movies, it may express nothing save the most perfect judgements and the utmost refinements of descriptivity and whet, nevertheless, no appetite for the unknown best, or for the best still unread by the neophyte.

A book 66 per cent concerned with manipulating and with rehandling the errors of seventy contemporary pestilential describers and rehashers of opinion, and only 34 per cent concerned with focusing the reader's attention on the *virtu* of books worth reading is, at least to the present victim, more an annoyance than a source of jocundity.

And if I am to put myself vicariously in the place of the younger reader or if I am to exercise parental protectiveness over some imagined offspring, I can find myself too angry for those mincing politenesses demanded by secondary editorial orders.

My opinion of critics is that:

The best are those who actually cause an amelioration in the art which they criticize.

The next best are those who most focus attention on the best that is written (or painted or composed or cut in stone).

And the pestilential vermin are those who distract

attention *from* the best, either to the second rate, or to hokum, or to their own critical writings.

Mr Eliot probably ranks very high in the first of these three groups, and deserves badly of us for his entrance into the last.

He uses Dryden legitimately in reducing exaggerated adulation of Milton, but the fact of his resurrecting Dryden poisons Professor Taupin, and so on *and* so on, thence further proceeding.

3

I don't at this point mean to criticize Taupin's *Quatres Essais*, but they offer me a fine chance to make an addendum.

Taupin is interesting while writing of Frobenius and Dante. In the latter case I suspect a Flamand ancestry has saved him from the n.r.f. dither and wish-wash. There is (naturally ?) a let down in the pages following. I suppose this is due to Taupin's respect for his elders. Professor Eliot in a fit of misanthropy dug up Dryden and Taupin was lured into reading him. The citation from Dryden may have been cleverly inserted by Taupin, at any rate it acts as a foil for his own somewhat contorted style to which one returns with relief from Dryden's platitude and verbosity. I am unable to determine whether Taupin is being superlatively astute and counting on the reader 'seeing for himself', or whether he was simply in a hurry, but 30 pages furnish a magnificent *basis* for deduction. Which he refrains from making. He may have expected the reader to see it for himself.

I know from longer experience than Dr René's that there is no use in expecting the reader to do anything of the sort. (No one has, for example, ever noticed the ground-plan of my *Instigations*.)

On page 161 Taupin quotes Condillac: 'Il y a deux espèces: le talent et le génie. Celui-là continue les idées d'un art ou d'une science connue, d'une manière propre à produire les effets qu'on en doit naturellement attendre …Celui-ci ajoute au talent l'idée d'esprit, en quelque sort créateur.'

Talent 'continues the ideas of a known art or science to produce naturally expectable results'.

On page 164 he quotes Milton: 'and twilight gray had in her sober livery all things clad'.

No one can be so ignorant as to suppose this manner of expression is anything save that of an art *known* and applied by several dozen dramatists. The Shakespearian original or model will instantly spring to the mind of almost any literate reader.

But the known process is vilely used. It is disgustingly used.

The Shakespearian line contains, I admit, one word not absolutely essential to the meaning. It is a mono-syllable and three of its four letters serve to concentrate and fulfil the double alliteration preceding.

Anybody but a botcher would have omitted the two useless words from the Milton. He not only derives but dilutes.

However, Taupin continues (still without heaving rocks at the victim) on the next page we find:

'the setting sun….'

PREFATIO AUT CIMICIUM TUMULUS

Gentlemen, ah wubb-wubb, what did the setting sun do?

'the setting sun.....

DESCENDED.'

The abject and utter nullity of British criticism in general for over two centuries is nowhere so squalid and naked as in the fact that generations of Britons and humble Americans have gone on swallowing this kind of rubbish. (Despite what Landor had shown them in his notes on Catullus.)

The only camouflage used to put over this idiocy is a gross and uninteresting rhythm.

The clodhoppers needed only one adverb between the subject and predicate to hide the underlying stupidity.

Chateaubriand, in a passage subsequently cited, was not, as Taupin seems to imply, supinely imitating the passage, but possibly trying to correct it, everything in his description is in place. His paragraph, like most so called prose poetry, lacks adequate rhythmic vitality and has, consequently, the dulness germane to its category.

MR ELIOT'S GRIEF

Mr Eliot's misfortune was to find himself surrounded by a horrible and microcephalous bureaucracy which disliked poetry, it might be too much to say 'loathed' it. But the emotion was as strong as any in the bureaucratic bosom. Bureaucracy has no loves and is composed mainly of varied minor dislikes. The members of this bureaucracy, sick with inferiority complex, had just enough wits to perceive that Eliot was their superior, but no means of detecting his limits or measuring him from the outside, and no experience that would enable them to know the poisons wherewith he had been injected. For that diagnosis perhaps only a fellow American is qualified, one having suffered an American University. The American University is or was aware of the existence of both German and English institutions, being younger and in a barbarous country, *its* inferiority complex impelled it to comparison and to a wish to equal and surpass, but gave it no immunity from the academical bacilli, inferiority complex directed against creative activity in the arts.

That there is a percentage of bunk in the *Selected Essays* Mr Eliot will possibly be the last to deny, but that he had performed a self-analysis is still doubtful.

This kind of essay assumes the existence of a culture that no longer subsists and does nothing to prepare a better culture that must or ought to come into being. I say 'better', for the new paideuma will at least be a live paideuma not a dead one.

Such essays are prepared NOT for editors who care about a living literature or a live tradition, or who even want the best of Eliot's perception applied to an author of second or third or fourth category (per ex. Seneca), they want to maintain a system wherein it is possible to receive fifteen guineas for an article of approximately 3000–4000 words, in a series to which Mr Eliot's sensitivity and patience will give lustre and wherein his occasional eminence will shed respectability on a great mass of inferior writing.

Their mentality is not far from that of a publisher of cheap editions who occasionally puts in a good book, so

that the serious German will think that the miscellany
is intellectual (*ipse dicebat*). Given the two or three real
books in his series he believes the German highbrow
will buy the rest thinking it the right thing to do.

IN HAPPIER ERA

The study of Latin authors was alive a century and
a quarter, perhaps hardly more than a century ago.

Young men are now lured into colleges and universities largely on false pretences.

We live in a vile age when it is impossible to get
reprints of the few dozen books that are practically
essential to a competent knowledge of poetry. When
Alexander Moring and Doctor Rouse set out to repub-
lish the books that had been good enough for Shakespeare, the enterprise went on the rocks. You can't get
a current edition of Golding's *Metamorphoses*, or of
Gavin Douglas, or of Salel; the British grocer will break
a contract for printing Cavalcanti when he would not
dream of breaking a contract for prunes.

In the matter of education, if the young are not to
profit by our sweats, if they are not to pluck the fruits
of our experience in the form of better curricula, it
might be well to give it up altogether. At any rate the
critic not aiming at a better curriculum for the serious
study of literature is a critic half-baked, swinging in a
vacuum. It would be hypocrisy to pretend that Eliot's
essays are not aimed at professors and students.

The student is best aided by being able to read and to
own conveniently the best that has been created.

Yeats, who has always been against the gang and the
bureaucracy, now muddled, now profound, now merely

Celtic or erroneously believing that a free Ireland, or at
least a more Oirish Ireland, would help the matter, long
ago prayed for a new sacred book.

Every age has tried to compound such a volume.
Every great culture has had such a major anthology.
Pisistratus, Li Po, the Japanese Emperor who reduced
the number of Noh dramas to about 450; the hackneyed
Hebrew example; in less degree the Middle Ages, with
the matter of Britain, of France, and of Rome le Grant.

The time to be interested in Seneca may possibly have
been before Mr Shakespeare had written his plays. But
assuming that Mr Eliot's plenum exists, the relations of
its different components have been changed in our time;
there are most distinctly the movies which bear on all
dramatic construction, and there are Max Ernst's few
volumes of engravings which have distinctly said their
word about the Freudian novel.

If the past 30 years have a meaning, that meaning is
not very apparent in Mr Eliot's condescensions to the
demands of British serial publication. If it means anything it means a distinct reduction in the BULK of past
literature that the future will carry.

I should have no right to attack England's most
accurate critic were it not in the hope of something
better, if not in England, at least somewhere in space
and time.

There is a habit or practice of attacking the lists in
How to Read. Young academes who have not read the
works listed say my choice is capricious, most of them
do not stop to see what my lists are lists OF.

I have catalogued the towns in Dorset without mentioning Durham. I have listed the cities in England and Scotland and omitted Berwick-on-Tweed. Therefore the assistant professor or the weekly reviewer is educated, superlatively educated, and I am still *impetuus juventus*, sipping with the bally bee and wholly unscientific in my methods.

Mr Aldington was perhaps the most vociferous, he vociferized about forty contradictions of things that I hadn't said, perhaps out of kindness, thinking it the only way his paper would give the booklet two columns, perhaps because he fawncied himself as the fine olde northern rough-haired St Bernard defending the kittens of Alexandria. He has always tended to lose his shirt and breeches if one made any restrictive remarks about Greeks, even though it were only to suggest that some Greeks wrote better than others.

Ut moveat, ut doceat, ut delectet.

There are at least three kinds of inaccurate statement which might with advantage be dissociated.

1. The somewhat violent statement conveying a perception (quia perception it is something perceived by the writer), the inaccuracy of such statement is often more apparent than real, and as every reader resists an opinion diverse from his own, such statement is often, one might say is usually, corrected or more than corrected in transit.

2. There is the apparently careful statement containing all the possible, or at least so many, modifications of the main proposition that the main meaning is either lost in transit or so dampened down that it has no effect on the reader.

Both these kinds of statement can be justified in

various ways depending on where and why they are used.

3. There is the inaccurate statement that is just simply vague, either because the writer doesn't KNOW or because he is incompetent in expression.

Such ignorance in successful vendors of their wares to current publications very often disguises itself as verity No. 2.

Camouflage might be further subdivided:

A. 'Sound opinion', i.e. restating accepted opinion without any direct or personal knowledge.

B. Covering this ignorance either with restrictive clauses, or scintillating with paradox.

There is gongorism in critical writing as well as in bad poetry. You might say that discussion of books ceases to be critical writing and becomes just the functioning of bureaucracy when the MAIN END (telos) is forgotten.

As we cannot educate our grandfathers, one supposes that critical writing is committed for the purpose of educating our offspring, our contemporaries, or ourselves, and that the least a critic can do is to be aware of the present even if he be too swinish to consider the future.

The critic is either a parasite or he is concerned with the growth of the next paideuma.

Marinetti is thoroughly *simpatico*. Writing and orating *ut moveat*, he has made demands that no one considers in their strict literal sense, but which have, and have had, a definite scope.

'An early play of no merit whatever', 'the brain of a fourth-rate playwright' as matters of an highly specialized clinic may conceivably have something to do with critical standards. The first impression is that their importance must be limited to some very minor philological field. Their import for to-morrow's paideuma is probably slight.

As specialist and practising writer one might want to know whether Seneca wrote any other lines as effective as

> Per alta vada spatia sublimi aethere
> testare nullos esse, qua veheris, deos.

Mr Eliot can think of no other play which reserves such a shock for the last word. (Ref. or cf. O. Henry's stories, bell in the last pages.)

The only trouble with the citation is that it is a bit ambiguous: Mr Eliot and Professor Miller disagreeing as to its theological import, Mr Eliot inclining to the Christian interpretation, or what Seneca ought to have meant. No, I musn't exaggerate. Seneca is not being Christian. Mr Eliot votes against a sweeping atheistical meaning. I can't personally see that the old half-bore goes further than asserting that the gods are not in that particular district of the æther. If there is anything about justice, it must be in the context, not in the two lines quoted.

In the present decomposition and under the yoke of the present bureaucracy it would probably be too much to demand that before discussing an author a reviewer answer the following questions:

1. Have you read the original text of the author under discussion? or how much of it have you read?

2. Is it worth reading? or how much of it is worth reading? and by whom?

As for Elizabethan dramedy, Lamb and Hazlitt are supposed to have set the fad, but Lamb at any rate did pick out a volume of selections; showing what he thought might be the basis of an interest.

The proportion between discussion and the exhibits the discusser dares show his reader is possibly a good, and probably a necessary, test of his purpose. In a matter of degree, I am for say 80 per cent exhibit and 20 per cent yatter.

Mr Eliot and Miss Moore are definitely fighting against an impoverishment of culture, against a paucity of reading programme. Neither they nor anyone else is likely to claim that they have as much interest in life as I have, or that I have their patience in reading.

That does not make it any less necessary to distinguish between Eliot registering his belief *re* a value, and Eliot ceding to the bad, not to say putrid habits of the bureaucracy which has surrounded him.

As alarmist, as capricious, perverse, etc., etc., I repeat that you cannot get the whole cargo of a sinking paideuma onto the lifeboat. If you propose to have any live literature of the past kept in circulation, available (flat materialism) in print at prices the eager reader can pay, there has got to be more attention to the best and to the basic. Once that is established you can divagate into marginalia, but the challenge will be more incisive and the criteria will be more rigorous.

In citing the Miltonic burble I am merely on my way towards a further assertion.

The critical sense shows more in composition than in a critical essay.

The unwelcome and disparate authors whom I have gathered in this volume have mostly accepted certain criteria which duller wits have avoided.

They have mostly, if not accepted, at any rate faced the demands, and considered the works, made and noted in my *How to Read*. That in itself is not a certificate of creative ability, but it does imply a freedom from certain forms of gross error and from certain kinds of bungling which will indubitably consign many other contemporary writings to the ash-bin, with more than expected celerity.

Mr Bunting probably seems reactionary to most of the other contributors. I think the apparent reaction is a definite endeavour to emphasize certain necessary elements which the less considering American experimentors tend to omit. At any rate Mr Bunting asserted that ambition some years ago, but was driven still further into the American ambience the moment he looked back upon British composition of, let us say, 1927–8.

I believe that Britain, in rejecting certain facts (facts, not opinions) in 1912–15 entered a sterile decade.

Willingness to experiment is not enough, but unwillingness to experiment is mere death.

If ten pages out of its two hundred and fifty go into a Corpus Poetarum of A.D. 2033, the present volume will amply be justified. (Yes, I know I have split the future of that verb. Var. will, and amply.)

I have not attempted to represent all the new poets, I am leaving the youngest, possibly some of the brightest, to someone else or to future effort, not so much from malice or objection to perfect justice, as from inability to do everything all at once.

There are probably fifty very bright poems that are not here assembled. I suspect Mr S. Putnam has written two or three. Mr Bridson is champing on the bit. Someone more in touch with the younger Americans ought to issue an anthology or a special number of some periodical, selected with *criteria*, either his or mine.

The assertion implicit in this volume is that after ten or twenty years of serious effort you can consider a writer uninteresting, but the charges of flightiness and dilettantism are less likely to be valid. In fact they are unlikely to be valid if a consistent direction can be discovered.

Other things being equal, the results of processes, even of secondary processes, application, patience, etc., are more pertinent from living writers than from dead ones, or are more pertinent when demonstrably IN RELATION with the living present than with the classified past.

Classic in current publishers' advertisements seems to have attained its meaning via classé, rangé.

The history of literature as taught in many institutions (? all) is nothing more (hardly more) than a stratified record of snobisms in which chronology sometimes counts for more than the causal relation and is also often wholly ignored, I mean ignored usually when it conflicts with prejudice and when chronological fact destroys a supposed causal relation.

I have resisted several temptations to reply to attacks on *How to Read*, because on examination the stricture was usually answered in my own text, and the attacker, had he been serious, could have found the correction where he assumed the fault. Several objectors (*ut ante*) simply have not taken the trouble to consider what my lists are lists of.

Others ignorant of the nature of some of the texts cited have assumed that they are not what they are.

Others have assumed that where, for sake of brevity, I have not given reasons for the inclusion of certain items, no reasons exist or can possibly.

Madox Ford made a serious charge, but not against what is on the pages of the booklet. He indicated that a section of what would be a more nearly complete treatise on the whole art of composition was not included. You can't get everything into 45 pages. Nor did the author of *How to Read* claim universal knowledge and competence. Neither in the title nor anywhere in the text did the booklet claim to be a treatise on the major structure of novels and epics, nor even a guide to creative composition.

As for experiment: the claim is that without constant experiment literature dies. Experiment is ONE of the elements necessary to its life. Experiment aims at writing that will have a relation to the present analogous to the relation which past masterwork had to the life of its time.

Eliot applying what he has learned from

    Morire.

        Cupio.

            Profugo.

                Paenitiunt fugae.

Medea.
         Fiam.
                  Mater es.
                           Cui sim vides.
applying what he has learned by being bored with as
much of the rest of Seneca as he has bothered to read, is
a vastly more vital Eliot, and a much more intensively
critical Eliot than when complying with the exigencies
of the present and verminous system for the excernment
of book-reviews.

I might also assert that Eliot going back to the original
has derived a vastly more vivid power than was possible
to the century and more of Elizafiers who were content
to lap the cream off Lamb and Hazlitt or to assume a
smattering of Elizabethan bumbast from Elizabethan
derivers. *Quod erat demonstrandum. Quod erat indicatum*,
even by the present disturber of repose anno 1917 and
thereabouts. And herein lies also the confutation of that
horrible *turba parasitorum paedagogorumque volgus* which
Mr Eliot tolerates in his vicinage.

'ACTIVE ANTHOLOGY'

A dislike of Bunting's poetry and Zukofsky's is possibly due to haste. Their verse is more thoughtful than toffee-lickers require. At intervals, months apart, I remember a passage, or I re-open my volume of excerpts and find something solid. It did not incinerate any Hudson river. Neither did Marianne Moore's when it first (20 years since) came to London. You have to read such verse slowly.

Apart from Bunting and Zukofsky, Miss Moore's is the solidest stuff in the Anthology. Williams' is simple by comparison—not so thoughtful. It has a larger audience because of its apparent simplicity. It is the lyric of an aptitude. Aptitude, not attitude. Anschauung, that Dr Williams has stuck in and to for half a century. The workmanship is not so much cared for. And yet Williams has become the first prose writer in America, the best prose writer who now gets into print, McAlmon having disappeared from circulation, and being a different case altogether, panoramic Velasquez, where Williams is just solid.

What goes into his case note is THERE. If there is any more solid solidity outside Papa Gustave, I don't know where to find it.

Joyce was not more substantial in the *Portrait of the*

Artist. I am not sure that the cutting hasn't lightened his block.

In his verse Williams' integrity passes for simplicity. Unadulterated non-elaboration in the phrase, a 'simple substance', simple has an analogous meaning; whereas Zukofsky, Bunting and Miss Moore are all thoughtful, much more so than the public desires.

'Man is not an end product', is much too condensed a phrase to tickle the gobbler.

The case of Cumming's "EIMI" and the bearing of Cocteau's sensibility on this discussion will have to wait further, and more thorough, treatment than I have given them. Mr Wyndham Lewis' *Apes* looms somewhere in the domain of Gulliver and Tristram Shandy.

HOW TO READ[1]

PART I: INTRODUCTION

*Largely Autobiographical, Touching the Present, and More or
Less Immediately Past, 'State of Affairs'.*

Literary instruction in our 'institutions of learning'
was, at the beginning of this century, cumbrous
and inefficient. I dare say it still is. Certain more
or less mildly exceptional professors were affected by
the 'beauties' of various authors (usually deceased), but
the system, as a whole, lacked sense and co-ordination.
I dare say it still does. When studying physics we are not
asked to investigate the biographies of all the disciples
of Newton who showed interest in science, but who
failed to make any discovery. Neither are their un-
rewarded gropings, hopes, passions, laundry bills, or
erotic experiences thrust on the hurried student or
considered germane to the subject.

The general contempt of 'scholarship', especially any
part of it connected with subjects included in university
'Arts' courses; the shrinking of people in general from
any book supposed to be 'good'; and, in another mode,
the flamboyant advertisements telling 'how to seem to
know it when you don't', might long since have indicated to the sensitive that there is something defective
in the contemporary methods of purveying letters.

[1] *New York Herald*, 'Books', 1928 or '27.

155

As the general reader has but a vague idea of what these methods are at the 'centre', i.e. for the specialist who is expected to serve the general reader, I shall lapse or plunge into autobiography.

In my university I found various men interested (or uninterested) in their subjects, but, I think, no man with a view of literature as a whole, or with any idea whatsoever of the relation of the part he himself taught to any other part.

Those professors who regarded their 'subject' as a drill manual rose most rapidly to positions of executive responsibility (one case is now a provost). Those professors who had some natural aptitude for comprehending their authors and for communicating a general sense of comfort in the presence of literary masterwork remained obscurely in their less exalted positions.

A professor of Romanics admitted that the *Chançon de Roland* was inferior to the *Odyssey*, but then the Middle Ages were expected to present themselves with apologies, and this was, if I remember rightly, an isolated exception. English novelists were not compared with the French. 'Sources' were discussed; forty versions of a Chaucerian anecdote were 'compared', but not on points of respective literary merit. The whole field was full of redundance. I mean that what one had learned in one class, in the study of one literature, one was told again in some other.

One was asked to remember what some critic (deceased) had said, scarcely to consider whether his views were still valid, or ever had been very intelligent.

In defence of this dead and uncorrelated system, it may be urged that authors like Spengler, who attempt

a synthesis, often do so before they have attained sufficient knowledge of detail: that they stuff expandable
and compressible objects into rubber-bag categories,
and that they limit their reference and interest by
supposing that the pedagogic follies which they have
themselves encountered, constitute an error universally
distributed, and encountered by every one else. In
extenuation of their miscalculations we may admit that
any error or clumsiness of method that has sunk into, or
been hammered into one man, over a period of years,
probably continues as an error—not merely passively,
but as an error still being propagated, consciously or
unconsciously, by a number of educators, from laziness,
from habit, or from natural cussedness.

'Comparative literature' sometimes figures in university curricula, but very few people know what they
mean by the term, or approach it with a considered
conscious method.

To tranquilize the low-brow reader, let me say at
once that I do not wish to muddle him by making him
read more books, but to allow him to read fewer with
greater result. (I am willing to discuss this privately
with the book trade.) I have been accused of wanting
to make people read all the classics; which is not so.
I have been accused of wishing to provide a 'portable
substitute for the British Museum', which I would do,
like a shot, were it possible. It isn't.

American 'taste' is less official than English taste, but
more derivative. When I arrived in England (A.D. 1908),
I found a greater darkness in the British 'serious press'
than had obtained on the banks of the Schuylkill.
Already in my young and ignorant years they con-

sidered me 'learned'. It was impossible, at first, to see why and whence the current opinion of British weeklies. It was incredible that literate men—men literate enough, that is, to write the orderly paragraphs that they did write constantly in their papers—believed the stupidities that appeared there with such regularity. (Later, for two years, we ran fortnightly in the *Egoist* the sort of fool-column that the French call a *sottisier*, needing nothing for it but quotations from the *Times Literary Supplement*. Two issues of the *Supplement* yielding, easily, one page of the *Egoist*). For years I awaited enlightenment. One winter I had lodgings in Sussex. On the mantelpiece of the humble country cottage I found books of an earlier era, among them an anthology printed in 1830, and yet another dated 1795, and there, there by the sox of Jehosaphat was the British taste of this century, 1910, 1915, and even the present, A.D. 1931.[1]

I had read Stendhal's remark that it takes eighty years for anything to reach the general public, and looking out on the waste heath, under the December drizzle, I believed him. But that is not all of the story. Embedded in that naive innocence that does, to their credit, pervade our universities, I ascribed the delay to mere time. I still thought: With the attrition of decades, ah, yes, in another seventy, in another, perhaps, ninety years, they will admit that...etc.

I mean that I thought they wanted to, but were hindered.

Later it struck me that the best history of painting in London was the National Gallery, and that the best history of literature, more particularly of poetry, would

[1] Date revised in reprint.

be a twelve-volume anthology in which each poem was chosen not merely because it was a nice poem or a poem Aunt Hepsy liked, but because it contained an invention, a definite contribution to the art of verbal expression. With this in mind, I approached a respected agent. He was courteous, he was even openly amazed at the list of three hundred items which I offered as an indication of outline. No autochthonous Briton had ever, to his professed belief, displayed such familiarity with so vast a range, but he was too indolent to recast my introductory letter into a form suited to commerce. He, as they say, 'repaired' to an equally august and long-established publishing house (which had already served his and my interest). In two days came a hasty summons: would I see him in person. I found him awed, as if one had killed a cat in the sacristy. Did I know what I had said in my letter? I did. Yes, but about Palgrave? I did. I had said: 'It is time we had something to replace that doddard Palgrave.' 'But don't you know', came the awestruck tones, 'that the whole fortune of X...& Co. is founded on Palgrave's *Golden Treasury*?'

From that day onward no book of mine received a British imprimatur until the appearance of Eliot's castrated edition of my poems.

I perceived that there were thousands of pounds sterling invested in electro-plate, and the least change in the public taste, let alone swift, catastrophic changes, would depreciate the value of those electros (of Hemans, let us say, or of Collins, Cowper, and of Churchill, who wrote the satiric verses, and of later less blatant cases, touched with a slighter flavour of mustiness).

I sought the banks of the Seine. Against ignorance

one might struggle, and even against organic stupidity, but against a so vast vested interest the lone odds were too heavy.

Two years later a still more august academic press reopened the question. *They* had ventured to challenge Palgrave; they had been 'interested'—would I send back my prospectus? I did. They found the plan 'too ambitious'. They said they might do 'something', but that if they did it would be 'more in the nature of gems'.

FOR A METHOD

Nevertheless, the method I had proposed was simple, it is perhaps the only one that can give a man an orderly arrangement of his perceptions in the matter of letters. In opposition to it, there are the forces of superstition, of hang-over. People regard literature as something vastly more flabby and floating and complicated and indefinite than, let us say, mathematics. Its subject-matter, the human consciousness, is more complicated than are number and space. It is not, however, more complicated than biology, and no one ever supposed that it was. We apply a loose-leaf system to book-keeping so as to have the live items separated from the dead ones. In the study of physics we begin with simple mechanisms, wedge, lever and fulcrum, pulley and inclined plane, all of them still as useful as when they were first invented. We proceed by a study of discoveries. We are not asked to memorize a list of the parts of a side-wheeler engine.

And we could, presumably, apply to the study of literature a little of the common sense that we currently apply to physics or to biology. In poetry there are simple procedures, and there are known discoveries, clearly marked. As I have said in various places in my unorganized and fragmentary volumes: in each age one or two men of genius find something, and express it. It may be in only a line or in two lines, or in some quality of a cadence; and thereafter two dozen, or two hundred, or two or more thousand followers repeat and dilute and modify.

And if the instructor would select his specimens from works that contain these discoveries and solely on the basis of discovery—which may lie in the dimension of depth, not merely of some novelty on the surface—he would aid his student far more than by presenting his authors at random, and talking about them *in toto*.

Needless to say, this presentation would be entirely independent of consideration as to whether the given passages tended to make the student a better republican, monarchist, monist, dualist, rotarian, or other sectarian. To avoid confusion, one should state at once that such method has nothing to do with those allegedly scientific methods which approach literature as if it were something *not literature*, or with scientists' attempts to subdivide the elements in literature according to some non-literary categoric division.

You do not divide physics or chemistry according to racial or religious categories. You do not put discoveries by Methodists and Germans into one category, and discoveries by Episcopalians or Americans or Italians into another.

DEFECTIVE RELATIVITIES

It is said that in America nothing is ever consciously related to anything else. I have cited as an exception the forty versions of the Chaucerian anecdote; they and the great edition of Horace with the careful list and parallel display of Greek sources for such line or such paragraph, show how the associative faculty can be side-tracked. Or at any rate they indicate the first gropings of association. Let us grant that some bits of literature have been, in special cases, displayed in relation to some other bits; usually some verbose gentleman writes a trilogy of essays, on three grandiose figures, comparing their 'philosophy' or personal habits.

Let us by all means glance at 'philology' and the 'germanic system'. Speaking as an historian, 'we' may say that this system was designed to inhibit thought. After 1848 it was, in Germany, observed that some people thought. It was necessary to curtail this pernicious activity, the thinkists were given a china egg labelled scholarship, and were gradually unfitted for active life, or for any contact with life in general. Literature was permitted as a subject of study. And its study was so designed as to draw the mind of the student away from literature into inanity.

WHY BOOKS?

I

This simple first question was never asked.

The study of literature, or more probably of morphology, verb-roots, etc., was permitted the German professor in, let us say, 1880–1905, to keep his mind off life in general, and off public life in particular.

In America it was permitted from precedent; it was known to be permitted in Germany; Germany had a 'great university tradition', which it behooved America to equal and perhaps to surpass.

This study, or some weaker variety of it, was also known to be permitted at Oxford, and supposed to have a refining influence on the student.

II

The practice of literary composition in private has been permitted since 'age immemorial', like knitting, crocheting, etc. It occupies the practitioner, and, so long as he keeps it to himself, *ne nuit pas aux autres*, it does not transgress the definition of liberty which we find in the declaration of the *Droits de l'Homme*: Liberty is the right to do anything which harms not others. All of which is rather negative and unsatisfactory.

III

It appears to me quite tenable that the function of literature as a generated prize-worthy force is precisely that it does incite humanity to continue living; that it eases the mind of strain, and feeds it, I mean definitely as *nutrition of impulse*.

This idea may worry lovers of order. Just as good literature does often worry them. They regard it as dangerous, chaotic, subversive. They try every idiotic and degrading wheeze to tame it down. They try to make a bog, a marasmus, a great putridity in place of a sane and active ebullience. And they do this from sheer simian and pig-like stupidity, and from their failure to understand the function of letters.

IV

Has literature a function in the state, in the aggregation of humans, in the republic, in the *res publica*, which ought to mean the public convenience (despite the slime of bureaucracy, and the execrable taste of the populace in selecting its rulers)? It has.

And this function is *not* the coercing or emotionally persuading, or bullying or suppressing people into the acceptance of any one set or any six sets of opinions as opposed to any other one set or half-dozen sets of opinions.

It has to do with the clarity and vigour of 'any and every' thought and opinion. It has to do with maintaining the very cleanliness of the tools, the health of the very matter of thought itself. Save in the rare and limited instances of invention in the plastic arts, or in mathematics, the individual cannot think and communicate his thought, the governor and legislator cannot act effectively or frame his laws, without words, and the solidity and validity of these words is in the care of the damned and despised *litterati*. When their work goes rotten—by that I do not mean when they express indecorous thoughts—but when their very medium, the very essence of their work, the application of word to thing goes rotten, i.e. becomes slushy and inexact, or excessive or bloated, the whole machinery of social and of individual thought and order goes to pot. This is a lesson of history, and a lesson not yet half learned.

The great writers need no debunking.

The pap is not in them, and doesn't need to be squeezed out. They do not lend themselves to imperial and sentimental exploitations. A civilization was founded on Homer, civilization not a mere bloated empire. The Macedonian domination rose and grew after the sophists. It also subsided.

It is not only a question of rhetoric, of loose expression, but also of the loose use of individual words. What the renaissance gained in direct examination of natural phenomena, it in part lost in losing the feel of and desire for exact descriptive terms. I mean that the medieval mind had little but words to deal with, and it was more careful in its definitions and verbiage. It did not define a gun in terms that would just as well define an explosion, nor explosions in terms that would define triggers.

Misquoting Confucius, one might say: It does not matter whether the author desire the good of the race or acts merely from personal vanity. The thing is mechanical in action. In proportion as his work is exact, i.e., true to human consciousness and to the nature of man, as it is exact in formulation of desire, so is it durable and so is it 'useful'; I mean it maintains the precision and clarity of thought, not merely for the benefit of a few dilettantes and 'lovers of literature', but maintains the health of thought outside literary circles and in non-literary existence, in general individual and communal life.

Or '*dans ce genre on n'émeut que par la clarté*'. One 'moves' the reader only by clarity. In depicting the motions of the 'human heart' the durability of the writing depends on the exactitude. It is the thing that is true and stays true that keeps fresh for the new reader.

With this general view in mind, and subsequent to the events already set forth in this narrative, I proposed (from the left bank of the Seine, and to an American publishing house), not the twelve-volume anthology, but a short guide to the subject. That was after a few years of 'pause and reflection'. The subject was pleasantly received and considered with amity, but the house finally decided that it would pay neither them to print nor me to write the book, because we 'weren't in the text-book ring'. For the thing would have been a text-book, its circulation would have depended on educators, and educators have been defined as 'men with no intellectual interests'.

Hence, after a lapse of four years, this essay, dedicated to Mr Glenn Frank, and other starters of ideal universities, though not with any great hope that it will rouse them.

PART II: OR WHAT MAY BE AN INTRODUCTION TO METHOD

It is as important for the purpose of thought to keep language efficient as it is in surgery to keep tetanus bacilli out of one's bandages.

In introducing a person to literature one would do well to have him examine works where language is efficiently used; to devise a system for getting directly and expeditiously at such works, despite the smoke-screens erected by half-knowing and half-thinking critics. To get at them, despite the mass of dead matter that these people have heaped up and conserved round about them in the proportion: one barrel of sawdust to each half-bunch of grapes.

Great literature is simply language charged with meaning to the utmost possible degree.

When we set about examining it we find that this charging has been done by several clearly definable sorts of people, and by a periphery of less determinate sorts.

(a) *The inventors*, discoverers of a particular process or of more than one mode and process. Sometimes these people are known, or discoverable; for example, we know, with reasonable certitude, that Arnaut Daniel introduced certain methods of rhyming, and we know that certain finenesses of perception appeared first in such a troubadour or in G. Cavalcanti. We do not know, and are not likely to know, anything definite about the precursors of Homer.

(b) *The masters*. This is a very small class, and there are very few real ones. The term is properly applied to inventors who, apart from their own inventions, are able to assimilate and co-ordinate a large number of preceding inventions. I mean to say they either start with a core of their own and accumulate adjuncts, or they digest a vast mass of subject-matter, apply a number of known modes of expression, and succeed in pervading the whole with some special quality or some special character of their own, and bring the whole to a state of homogeneous fulness.

(c) *The diluters*, those who follow either the inventors or the 'great writers', and who produce something of lower intensity, some flabbier variant, some diffuseness or tumidity in the wake of the valid.

(d) (And this class produces the great bulk of all

writing.) The men who do more or less good work in the more or less good style of a period. Of these the delightful anthologies, the song books, are full, and choice among them is the matter of taste, for you prefer Wyatt to Donne, Donne to Herrick, Drummond of Hawthornden to Browne, in response to some purely personal sympathy, these people add but some slight personal flavour, some minor variant of a mode, without affecting the main course of the story.

At their faintest '*Ils n'existent pas, leur ambiance leur confert une existence.*' They do not exist: their ambience confers existence upon them. When they are most prolific they produce dubious cases like Virgil and Petrarch, who probably pass, among the less exigeant, for colossi.

(*e*) *Belles Lettres.* Longus, Prévost, Benjamin Constant, who are not exactly 'great masters', who can hardly be said to have originated a form, but who have nevertheless brought some mode to a very high development.

(*f*) And there is a supplementary or sixth class of writers, the starters of crazes, the Ossianic McPhersons, the Gongoras whose wave of fashion flows over writing for a few centuries or a few decades, and then subsides, leaving things as they were.

It will be seen that the first two classes are the more sharply defined: that the difficulty of classification for particular lesser authors increases as one descends through the list, save for the last class, which is again fairly clear.

The point is, that if a man know the facts about the first two categories, he can evaluate almost any unfamiliar book at first sight. I mean he can form a just estimate of its worth, and see how and where it belongs in this schema.

As to crazes, the number of possible diseases in literature is perhaps not very great, the same afflictions crop up in widely separated countries without any previous communication. The good physician will recognize a known malady, even if the manifestation be superficially different.

The fact that six different critics will each have a different view concerning what author belongs in which of the categories here given, does not in the least invalidate the categories. When a man knows the facts about the first two categories, the reading of work in the other categories will not greatly change his opinion about those in the first two.

LANGUAGE

Obviously this knowledge cannot be acquired without knowledge of various tongues. The same discoveries have served a number of races. If a man have not time to learn different languages he can at least, and with very little delay, be told what the discoveries were. If he wish to be a good critic he will have to look for himself.

Bad critics have prolonged the use of demoded terminology, usually a terminology originally invented to describe what had been done before 300 B.C., and to describe it in a rather exterior fashion. Writers of second order have often tried to produce works to fit some category or term not yet occupied in their own local literature. If we chuck out the classifications which apply to the outer shape of the work, or to its occasion, and if we look at what actually happens, in, let us say, poetry, we will find that the language is charged or energized in various manners.

That is to say, there are three 'kinds of poetry':

MELOPŒIA, wherein the words are charged, over and above their plain meaning, with some musical property, which directs the bearing or trend of that meaning.

PHANOPŒIA, which is a casting of images upon the visual imagination.

LOGOPŒIA, 'the dance of the intellect among words', that is to say, it employs words not only for their direct meaning, but it takes count in a special way of habits of usage, of the context we *expect* to find with the word, its usual concomitants, of its known acceptances, and of ironical play. It holds the aesthetic content which is peculiarly the domain of verbal manifestation, and cannot possibly be contained in plastic or in music. It is the latest come, and perhaps most tricky and undependable mode.

The *melopœia* can be appreciated by a foreigner with a sensitive ear, even though he be ignorant of the language in which the poem is written. It is practically impossible to transfer or translate it from one language to another, save perhaps by divine accident, and for half a line at a time.

Phanopœia can, on the other hand, be translated almost, or wholly, intact. When it is good enough, it is practically impossible for the translator to destroy it save by very crass bungling, and the neglect of perfectly well-known and formulatable rules.

Logopœia does not translate; though the attitude of mind it expresses may pass through a paraphrase. Or one might say, you can *not* translate it 'locally', but having determined the original author's state of mind, you may or may not be able to find a derivative or an equivalent.

PROSE

The language of prose is much less highly charged, that is perhaps the only availing distinction between prose and poesy. Prose permits greater factual presentation, explicitness, but a much greater amount of language is needed. During the last century or century and a half, prose has, perhaps for the first time, perhaps for the second or third time, arisen to challenge the poetic pre-eminence. That is to say, *Cœur Simple*, by Flaubert, is probably more important than Théophile Gautier's *Carmen*, etc.

The total charge in certain nineteenth-century prose works possibly surpasses the total charge found in individual poems of that period; but that merely indicates that the author has been able to get his effect cumulatively, by a greater heaping up of factual data; imagined fact, if you will, but nevertheless expressed in factual manner.

By using several hundred pages of prose, Flaubert, by force of architectonics, manages to attain an intensity comparable to that in Villon's *Heaulmière*, or his prayer for his mother. This does not invalidate my dissociation of the two terms: poetry, prose.

In *phanopœia* we find the greatest drive toward utter precision of word; this art exists almost exclusively by it.

In *melopœia* we find a contrary current, a force tending often to lull, or to distract the reader from the exact sense of the language. It is poetry on the borders of music, and music is perhaps the bridge between consciousness and the unthinking sentient or even insentient universe.

All writing is built up of these three elements, plus 'architectonics' or 'the form of the whole', and to know anything about the relative efficiency of various works one must have some knowledge of the maximum already attained by various authors, irrespective of where and when.[1]

It is not enough to know that the Greeks attained to the greatest skill in *melopœia*, or even that the Provençaux added certain diverse developments and that some quite minor, nineteenth-century Frenchmen achieved certain elaborations.

It is not quite enough to have the general idea that the Chinese (more particularly Rihaku and Omakitsu) attained the known maximum of *phanopœia*, due perhaps to the nature of their written ideograph, or to wonder whether Rimbaud is, at rare moments, their equal. One wants one's knowledge in more definite terms.

It is an error to think that vast reading will automatically produce any such knowledge or understanding. Neither Chaucer with his forty books, nor Shakespeare with perhaps half a dozen, in folio, can be considered illiterate. A man can learn more music by working on a Bach fugue until he can take it apart and put it together, than by playing through ten dozen heterogeneous albums.

You may say that for twenty-seven years I have

---

[1] Lacuna at this point to be corrected in criticism of Hindemith's "Schwanendreher". E. P. Sept. 1936.

thought consciously about this particular matter, and read or read at a great many books, and that with the subject never really out of my mind, I don't yet know half there is to know about *melopœia*.

There are, on the other hand, a few books that I still keep on my desk, and a great number that I shall never open again. But the books that a man needs to know in order to 'get his bearings', in order to have a sound judgment of any bit of writing that may come before him, are very few. The list is so short, indeed, that one wonders that people, professional writers in particular, are willing to leave them ignored and to continue dangling in mid-chaos emitting the most imbecile estimates, and often vitiating their whole lifetime's production.

Limiting ourselves to the authors who actually invented something, or who are the 'first known examples' of the process in working order, we find:

OF THE GREEKS: Homer, Sappho. (The 'great dramatists' decline from Homer, and depend immensely on him for their effects; their 'charge', at its highest potential, depends so often, and so greatly on their being able to count on their audience's knowledge of the *Iliad*. Even Æschylus is rhetorical.)

OF THE ROMANS: As we have lost Philetas, and most of Callimachus, we may suppose that the Romans added a certain sophistication; at any rate, Catullus, Ovid, Propertius, all give us something we cannot find now in Greek authors.

A specialist may read Horace if he is interested in learning the precise demarcation between what can be learned about writing, and what cannot. I mean that

Horace is the perfect example of a man who acquired all that is acquirable, without having the root. I beg the reader to observe that I am being exceedingly icono-clastic, that I am omitting thirty established names for every two I include. I am chucking out Pindar, and Virgil, without the slightest compunction. I do not suggest a 'course' in Greek or Latin literature, I name a few isolated writers; five or six pages of Sappho. One can throw out at least one-third of Ovid. That is to say, I am omitting the authors who can teach us no new or no more effective method of 'charging' words.

OF THE MIDDLE AGES: The Anglo-Saxon *Seafarer*, and some more cursory notice of some medieval nar-rative, it does not so greatly matter what narrative, possibly the *Beowulf*, the *Poema del Cid*, and the sagas of *Grettir* and *Burnt Nial*. And then, in contrast, trouba-dours, perhaps thirty poems in Provençal, and for comparison with them a few songs by Von Morungen, or Wolfram von Essenbach, and von der Vogelweide; and then Bion's *Death of Adonis*.

From which mixture, taken in this order, the reader will get his bearings on the art of poetry made to be sung; for there are three kinds of *melopœia*: (1) that made to be sung to a tune; (2) that made to be intoned or sung to a sort of chant; and (3) that made to be spoken; and the art of joining words in each of these kinds is different, and cannot be clearly understood until the reader knows that there are three different objectives.

OF THE ITALIANS: Guido Cavalcanti and Dante; perhaps a dozen and a half poems of Guido's, and a dozen poems by his contemporaries, and the *Divina Commedia*.

In Italy, around the year 1300, there were new values

established, things said that had not been said in Greece, or in Rome or elsewhere.

VILLON: After Villon and for several centuries, poetry can be considered as *fioritura*, as an efflorescence, almost an effervescence, and without any new roots. Chaucer is an enrichment, one might say a more creamy version of the 'matter of France', and he in some measure preceded the verbal richness of the classic revival, but beginning with the Italians after Dante, coming through the Latin writers of the Renaissance, French, Spanish, English, Tasso, Ariosto, etc., the Italians always a little in the lead, the whole is elaboration, medieval basis, and wash after wash of Roman or Hellenic influence. I mean one need not read any particular part of it for purpose of learning one's comparative values.

If one were studying history and not poetry, one might discover the medieval mind more directly in the opening of Mussato's *Ecerinus* than even in Dante. The culture of Chaucer is the same which went contemporaneously into Ferrara, with the tongue called '*francoveneto*'.

One must emphasize one's contrasts in the quattrocento. One can take Villon as pivot for understanding them. After Villon, and having begun before his time, we find this *fioritura*, and for centuries we find little else. Even in Marlowe and Shakespeare there is this embroidery of language, this talk about the matter, rather than presentation. I doubt if anyone ever acquired discrimination in studying 'The Elizabethans'. You have grace, richness of language, abundance, but you have probably nothing that isn't replaceable by something else, no ornament that wouldn't have done just as well in some other connection, or for which some other figure of rhetoric couldn't have served, or which couldn't have been distilled from literary antecedents.

The 'language' had not been heard on the London stage, but it had been heard in the Italian law courts, etc.; there were local attempts, all over Europe, to teach the public (in Spain, Italy, England) Latin diction. 'Poetry' was considered to be (as it still is considered by a great number of drivelling imbeciles) synonymous with 'lofty and flowery language'.

One Elizabethan specialist has suggested that Shakespeare, disgusted with his efforts, or at least despairing of success, as a poet, took to the stage. The drama is a mixed art; it does not rely on the charge that can be put into the word, but calls on gesture and mimicry and 'impersonation' for assistance. The actor must do a good half of the work. One does no favour to drama by muddling the two sets of problems.

Apologists for the drama are continually telling us in one way or another that drama either cannot use at all, or can make but a very limited use of words charged to their highest potential. This is perfectly true. Let us try to keep our minds on the problem we started with, i.e., the art of writing, the art of 'charging' language with meaning.

After 1450 we have the age of *fioritura*; after Marlowe and Shakespeare came what was called a 'classic' movement, a movement that restrained without inventing. Anything that happens to mind in England has usually happened somewhere else first. Someone invents something, then someone develops, or some dozens develop a frothy or at any rate creamy enthusiasm or over-abundance, then someone tries to tidy things up. For example, the estimable Pleiad emasculating the French tongue, and the French classicists, and the English classicists, etc., all of which things should be relegated to the subsidiary zone: period interest, historical interest, bric-à-brac for museums.

At this point someone says: 'O, but the ballads.' All right, I will allow the voracious peruser a half-hour for ballads (English and Spanish, or Scotch, Border, and Spanish). There is nothing easier than to be distracted from one's point, or from the main drive of one's subject by a desire for utterly flawless equity and omniscience.

Let us say, but strictly in parenthesis, that there was a very limited sort of *logopœia* in seventeenth- and eighteenth-century satire. And that Rochester and Dorset may have introduced a new note, or more probably re-introduced an old one, that reappears later in Heine.

Let us also cut loose from minor details and minor exceptions: the main fact is that we 'have come' or that 'humanity came' to a point where verse-writing can or could no longer be clearly understood without the study of prose-writing.

Say, for the sake of argument, that after the slump of the Middle Ages, prose 'came to' again in Machiavelli; admit that various sorts of prose had existed, in fact nearly all sorts had existed. Herodotus wrote history that is literature, Thucydides was a journalist. (It is a modern folly to suppose that vulgarity and cheapness have the merit of novelty; they have always existed, and are of no interest in themselves.)

There had been bombast, oratory, legal speech, balanced sentences, Ciceronian impressiveness; Petronius had written a satiric novel, Longus had written a delicate nouvelle. The prose of the Renaissance leaves us Rabelais, Brantôme, Montaigne. A determined specialist can dig interesting passages, or sumptuous passages, or even subtle passages out of Pico, the medieval mystics, scholastics, platonists, none of which will be the least use to a man trying to learn the art of 'charging language'.

I mean to say that from the beginning of literature up to 1750 A.D., poetry was the superior art, and was so considered to be, and if we read books written before that date we find the number of interesting books in verse at least equal to the number of prose books still readable; and the poetry contains the quintessence. When we want to know what people were like before 1750, when we want to know that they had blood and bones like ourselves, we go to the poetry of the period.

But, as I have said, this '*fioritura* business' set in. And one morning Monsieur Stendhal, not thinking of Homer, or Villon, or Catullus, but having a very keen sense of actuality, noticed that 'poetry', *la poésie*, as the term was then understood, the stuff written by his French contemporaries, or sonorously rolled at him from the French stage, was a damn nuisance. And he remarked that poetry, with its bagwigs and its bobwigs, and its padded calves and its periwigs, its 'fustian à la Louis XIV', was greatly inferior to prose for conveying a clear idea of the diverse states of our consciousness ('*les mouvements de cœur*').

And at that moment the serious art of writing 'went over to prose', and for some time the important developments of language as means of expression were the developments of prose. And a man cannot clearly understand or justly judge the value of verse, modern verse, any verse, unless he have grasped this.

PART III: CONCLUSIONS, EXCEPTIONS, CURRICULA

Before Stendhal there is probably nothing in prose that does not also exist in verse or that can't be done by verse just as well as by prose. Even the method of annihilating imbecility employed by Voltaire, Bayle, and Lorenzo Valla can be managed quite as well in rhymed couplets.

Beginning with the Renaissance, or perhaps with Boccaccio, we have prose that is quite necessary to the clear comprehension of things in general: with Rabelais, Brantôme, Montaigne, Fielding, Sterne, we begin to find prose recording states of consciousness that their verse-writing contemporaries scamp. And this fuller consciousness, in more delicate modes, appears in l'Abbé Prévost, Benjamin Constant, Jane Austen. So that Stendhal had already 'something back of him' when he made his remarks about the inferiority of '*La Poésie*'.

During the nineteenth century the superiority, if temporary, is at any rate obvious, and to such degree that I believe no man can now write really good verse unless he knows Stendhal and Flaubert. Or, let us say,

Le Rouge et le Noir, the first half of *La Chartreuse*, *Madame Bovary*, *L'Éducation*, *Les Trois Contes*, *Bouvard et Pécuchet*. To put it perhaps more strongly, he will learn more about the art of charging words from Flaubert than he will from the floribund sixteenth-century dramatists.

The main expression of nineteenth-century consciousness is in prose. The art continues in Maupassant, who slicked up the Flaubertian mode. The art of popular success lies simply in never putting more on any one page than the most ordinary reader can lick off it in his normally rapid, half-attentive skim-over. The Goncourts struggled with praiseworthy sobriety, noble, but sometimes dull. Henry James was the first person to add anything to the art of the nineteenth-century novel not already known to the French.

Thought was churned up by Darwin, by science, by industrial machines, Nietzsche made a temporary commotion, but these things are extraneous to our subject, which is the *art of getting meaning into words*. There is an 'influence of Ibsen', all for the good, but now exploited by cheap-jacks. Fabre and Frazer are both essential to contemporary clear thinking. I am not talking about the books that have poured something into the general consciousness, but of books that show *how* the pouring is done or display the implements, newly discovered, by which one can pour.

The nineteenth-century novel is such an implement. The Ibsen play is, or perhaps we must say was, such an implement.

It is for us to think whether these implements are more effective than poetry: (*a*) as known before 1800; (*b*) as known during the nineteenth century and up to the present.

FRANCE

The decline of England began on the day when Landor packed his trunks and departed to Tuscany. Up till then England had been able to contain her best authors; after that we see Shelley, Keats, Byron, Beddoes on the Continent, and still later observe the edifying spectacle of Browning in Italy and Tennyson in Buckingham Palace.

In France, as the novel developed, spurred on, shall we say, by the activity in the prose-media, the versifiers were not idle.

Departing from *Albertus*, Gautier developed the medium we find in the *Émaux et Camées*. England in the 'nineties had got no further than the method of the *Albertus*. If Corbière invented no process he at any rate restored French verse to the vigour of Villon and to an intensity that no Frenchman had touched during the intervening four centuries.

Unless I am right in discovering *logopœia* in Propertius (which means unless the academic teaching of Latin displays crass insensitivity, as it probably does), we must almost say that Laforgue invented *logopœia*—observing that there had been a very limited range of *logopœia* in all satire, and that Heine occasionally employs something like it, together with a dash of bitters, such as can (though he may not have known it) be found in a few verses of Dorset and Rochester. At any rate Laforgue found or refound *logopœia*. And Rimbaud brought back to *phanopœia* its clarity and directness.

All four of these poets, Gautier, Corbière, Laforgue, Rimbaud, redeem poetry from Stendhal's condemnation. There is in Corbière something one finds nowhere before him, unless in Villon.

Laforgue is not like any preceding poet. He is not ubiquitously like Propertius.

In Rimbaud the image stands clean, unencumbered by non-functioning words; to get anything like this directness of presentation one must go back to Catullus, perhaps to the poem which contains *dentes habet*.

If a man is too lazy to read the brief works of these poets, he cannot hope to understand writing, verse writing, prose writing, any writing.

ENGLAND

Against this serious action England can offer only Robert Browning. He has no French or European parallel. He has, indubitably, grave limitations, but *The Ring and the Book* is serious experimentation. He is a better poet than Landor, who was perhaps the only complete and serious man of letters ever born in these islands.

We are so encumbered by having British literature in our foreground that even in this brief survey one must speak of it in disproportion. It was kept alive during the last century by a series of exotic injections. Swinburne read Greek and took English metric in hand; Rossetti brought in the Italian primitives; FitzGerald made the only good poem of the time that has gone to the people; it is called, and is to a great extent, a trans- or mistrans-lation.

There was a faint waft of early French influence.

Morris translated sagas, the Irish took over the business for a few years; Henry James led, or rather preceded, the novelists, and then the Britons resigned *en bloc*; the language is now in the keeping of the Irish (Yeats and Joyce); apart from Yeats, since the death of Hardy, poetry is being written by Americans. All the developments in English verse since 1910 are due almost wholly to Americans. In fact, there is no longer any reason to call it English verse, and there is no present reason to think of England at all.

We speak a language that was English. When Richard Cœur de Lion first heard Turkish he said: 'He spik lak a fole Britain.' From which orthography one judges that Richard himself probably spoke like a French-Canadian.

It is a magnificent language, and there is no need of, or advantage in, minimizing the debt we owe to Englishmen who died before 1620. Neither is there any point in studying the 'History of English Literature' as taught. Curiously enough, the histories of Spanish and Italian literature always take count of translators. Histories of English literature always slide over translation—I suppose it is inferiority complex—yet some of the best books in English are translations. This is important for two reasons. First, the reader who has been appalled by the preceding parts and said, 'Oh, but I can't learn all these languages', may in some measure be comforted. He can learn the art of writing precisely where so many great local lights learned it; if not from the definite poems I have listed, at least from the men who learned it from those poems in the first place.

We may count the *Seafarer*, the *Beowulf*, and the

remaining Anglo-Saxon fragments as indigenous art; at least, they dealt with a native subject, and by an art not newly borrowed. Whether alliterative metre owes anything to Latin hexameter is a question open to debate; we have no present means of tracing the debt. Landor suggests the problem in his dialogue of Ovid and the Prince of the Gaetæ.

After this period English literature lives on translation, it is fed by translation; every new exuberance, every new heave is stimulated by translation, every allegedly great age is an age of translations, beginning with Geoffrey Chaucer, Le Grand Translateur, translator of the *Romaunt of the Rose*, paraphraser of Virgil and Ovid, condenser of old stories he had found in Latin, French, and Italian.

After him even the ballads that tell a local tale tell it in art indebted to Europe. It is the natural spreading ripple that moves from the civilized Mediterranean centre out through the half-civilized and into the barbarous peoples.

The Britons never have shed barbarism; they are proud to tell you that Tacitus said the last word about Germans. When Mary Queen of Scots went to Edinburgh she bewailed going out among savages, and she herself went from a sixteenth-century court that held but a barbarous, or rather a drivelling and idiotic and superficial travesty of the Italian culture as it had been before the débâcle of 1527. The men who tried to civilize these shaggy and uncouth marginalians by bringing them news of civilization have left a certain number of translations that are better reading to-day than are the works of the ignorant islanders who were too proud to

translate. After Chaucer we have Gavin Douglas's
Eneados, better than the original, as Douglas had heard
the sea. Golding's *Metamorphoses*, from which Shakespeare learned so much of his trade. Marlowe's translation of Ovid's *Amores*. We have no satisfactory translation of any Greek author. Chapman and Pope have
left Iliads that are of interest to specialists; so far as I
know, the only translation of Homer that one can read
with continued pleasure is in early French by Hugues
Salel; he, at least, was intent on telling the story, and
not wholly muddled with accessories. I have discussed
the merits of these translators elsewhere. I am now
trying to tell the reader what he can learn of comparative
literature through translations that are in themselves
better reading than the 'original verse' of their periods.
He can study the whole local development, or, we had
better say, the sequence of local fashion in British verse
by studying the translations of Horace that have poured
in uninterrupted sequence from the British press since
1650. That is work for a specialist, an historian, not for
a man who wants simply to establish his axes of reference
by knowing *the best of each kind* of written thing; as he
would establish his axes of reference for painting by
knowing a few pictures by Cimabue, Giotto, Piero della
Francesca, Ambrogio de Predis, etc.; Velasquez, Goya,
etc.

It is one thing to be able to spot the best painting and
quite another and far less vital thing to know just where
some secondary or tertiary painter learned certain defects.

Apart from these early translations, a man may
enlarge his view of international poetry by looking at

Swinburne's Greek adaptations. The Greeks stimulated Swinburne; if he had defects, let us remember that, apart from Homer, the Greeks often were rather Swinburnian. Catullus wasn't, or was but seldom. From which one may learn the nature of the Latin, non-Greek contribution to the art of expression.

Swinburne's Villon is not Villon very exactly, but it is perhaps the best Swinburne we have. Rossetti's translations were perhaps better than Rossetti, and his *Vita Nuova* and early Italian poets guide one to originals, which he has now and again improved. Our contact with Oriental poetry begins with FitzGerald's *Rubáiyát*. Fenollosa's essay on the Chinese written character opens a door that the earlier students had, if not 'howled without', at least been unable to open.

In mentioning these translations, I don't in the least admit or imply that any man in our time can think with only one language. He may be able to invent a new carburettor, or even work effectively in a biological laboratory, but he probably won't even try to do the latter without study of at least one foreign tongue. Modern science has always been multilingual. A good scientist simply would not be bothered to limit himself to one language and be held up for news of discoveries. The writer or reader who is content with such ignorance simply admits that his particular mind is of less importance than his kidneys or his automobile. The French who know no English are as fragmentary as the Americans who know no French. One simply leaves half of one's thought untouched in their company.

Different languages—I mean the actual vocabularies, the idioms—have worked out certain mechanisms of communication and registration. No one language is complete. A master may be continually expanding his own tongue, rendering it fit to bear some charge hitherto borne only by some other alien tongue, but the process does not stop with any one man. While Proust is learning Henry James, preparatory to breaking through certain French paste-board partitions, the whole American speech is churning and chugging, and every other tongue doing likewise.

To be 'possible' in mentally active company the American has to learn French, the Frenchman has to learn English or American. The Italian has for some time learned French. The man who does not know the Italian of the duocento and trecento has in him a painful lacuna, not necessarily painful to himself, but there are simply certain things he don't know, and can't; it is as if he were blind to some part of the spectrum. Because of the determined attempt of the patriotic Latinists of Italy in the renaissance to 'conquer' Greek by putting every Greek author effectively into Latin it is now possible to get at a good deal of Greek through Latin cribs. The disuse of Latin cribs in Greek study, beginning, I suppose, about 1820, has caused no end of damage to the general distribution of 'classic culture'.

Another point miscomprehended by people who are clumsy at languages is that one does not need to learn a whole language in order to understand some one or some dozen poems. It is often enough to understand thoroughly the poem, and every one of the few dozen or few hundred words that compose it.

This is what we start to do as small children when we memorize some lyric of Goethe or Heine. Incidentally, this process leaves us for life with a measuring rod (*a*) for a certain type of lyric, (*b*) for the German language, so that, however bored we may be by the *Grundriss von Groeber*, we never wholly forget the feel of the language.

VACCINE

Do I suggest a remedy? I do. I suggest several remedies. I suggest that we throw out all critics who use vague general terms. Not merely those who use vague terms because they are too ignorant to have a meaning; but the critics who use vague terms to *conceal* their meaning, and all critics who use terms so vaguely that the reader can think he agrees with them or assents to their statements when he doesn't.

The first credential we should demand of a critic is *his* ideograph of the good; of what he considers valid writing, and indeed of all his general terms. Then we know where he is. He cannot simply stay in London writing of French pictures that his readers have not seen. He must begin by stating that such and such *particular* works seem to him 'good', 'best', 'indifferent', 'valid', 'non-valid'. I suggest a definite curriculum in place of the present *émiettements*, of breaking the subject up into crumbs quickly dryable. A curriculum for instructors, for obstreperous students who wish to annoy dull instructors, for men who haven't had time for systematized college courses. Call it the minimum basis for a sound and liberal education in letters (with French and English 'aids' in parenthesis).

CONFUCIUS—In full (there being no complete and

intelligent English version, one would have either to learn Chinese or make use of the French version by Pauthier).

HOMER—In full (Latin cribs, Hugues Salel in French, no satisfactory English, though Chapman can be used as reference).

OVID—And the Latin 'personal' poets, Catullus and Propertius. (Golding's *Metamorphoses*, Marlowe's *Amores*. There is no useful English version of Catullus.)

A PROVENÇAL SONG BOOK—With cross reference to Minnesingers, and to Bion, perhaps thirty poems in all.

DANTE—'And his circle'; that is to say Dante, and thirty poems by his contemporaries, mostly by Guido Cavalcanti.

VILLON—

PARENTHETICALLY—Some other medieval matter might be added, and some general outline of history of thought through the Renaissance.

VOLTAIRE—That is to say, some incursion into his critical writings, not into his attempts at fiction and drama, and some dip into his contemporaries (prose).

STENDHAL—(At least a book and half).

FLAUBERT (omitting *Salammbô* and the *Tentation*)— And the Goncourts.

GAUTIER, CORBIÈRE, RIMBAUD.

This would not overburden the three- or four-year student. After this inoculation he could be 'with safety exposed' to modernity or anything else in literature. I mean he wouldn't lose his head or ascribe ridiculous values to works of secondary intensity. He would have axes of reference and, would I think, find them dependable.

For the purposes of general education we could omit all study of monistic totemism and voodoo for at least fifty years and study of Shakespeare for thirty on the ground that acquaintance with these subjects is already very widely diffused, and that one absorbs quite enough knowledge of them from boring circumjacent conversation.

This list does not, obviously, contain the names of every author who has ever written a good poem or a good octave or sestet. It is the result of twenty-seven years' thought on the subject and a résumé of conclusions. That may be a reason for giving it some consideration. It is not a reason for accepting it as a finality. Swallowed whole it is useless. For practical class work the instructor should try, and incite his students to try, to pry out some element that I have included and to substitute for it something more valid. The intelligent lay reader will instinctively try to do this for himself.

I merely insist that *without* this minimum the critic has almost no chance of sound judgment. Judgment will gain one more chance of soundness if he can be persuaded to consider Fenollosa's essay or some other, and to me unknown but equally effective, elucidation of the Chinese written character.

Before I die I hope to see at least a few of the best Chinese works printed bilingually, in the form that Mori and Ariga prepared certain texts for Fenollosa, a 'crib', the picture of each letter accompanied by a full explanation.

For practical contact with all past poetry that was

actually *sung* in its own day I suggest that each dozen universities combine in employing a couple of singers who understand the meaning of words. Men like Yves Tinayre and Robert Maitland are available. A half-dozen hours spent in listening to the lyrics actually performed would give the student more knowledge of that sort of *melopœia* than a year's work in philology. The Kennedy-Frasers have dug up music that fits the *Beowulf*. It was being used for heroic song in the Hebrides. There is other available music, plenty of it, from at least the time of Faidit (A.D. 1190).

I cannot repeat too often or too forcibly my caution against so-called critics who talk 'all around the matter', and who do not define their terms, and who won't say frankly that certain authors are demnition bores. Make a man tell you *first* and specially what writers he thinks are good writers, after that you can listen to his explanation.

Naturally, certain professors who have invested all their intellectual capital, i.e., spent a lot of time on some perfectly dead period, don't like to admit they've been sold, and they haven't often the courage to cut a loss. There is no use in following them into the shadows.

In the above list I take full responsibility for my omissions. I have omitted 'the Rhooshuns' all right. Let a man judge them after he has encountered Charles Bovary; he will read them with better balance. I have omitted practically all the fustian included in curricula of French literature in American universities (Bossuet, Corneille, etc.) and in so doing I have not committed an oversight. I have touched German in what most of you will consider an insufficient degree. All right. I have done it. I rest my case.

If one finds it convenient to think in chronological cycles, and wants to 'relate literature to history', I suggest the three convenient 'breaks' or collapses. The fall of Alexander's Macedonian empire; the fall of the Roman empire; the collapse of Italy after 1500, the fall of Lodovico Moro, and the sack of Rome. That is to say, human lucidity appears to have approached several times a sort of maximum, and then suffered a set-back.

The great break in the use of language occurs, however, with the change from inflected to uninflected speech. It can't be too clearly understood that certain procedures are good for a language in which every word has a little final tag telling what part of speech it is, and what case it is in, and whether it is a subject, or an object or an accessory; and that these procedures are not good in English or French. Milton got into a mess trying to write English as if it were Latin. Lack of this dissociation is largely responsible for late renaissance floridity. One cannot at this point study all the maladies and all their variations. The study of misguided Latinization needs a treatise to itself.[1]

[1] Argument of this essay is elaborated in the author's *ABC of Reading*.

CIVILIZATION

I

Honesty of the word does not permit dishonesty
of the matter

If in my early criticism I showed a just contempt for the falsity of writers who would not face technical problems, that cannot pass, for much longer, as indifference to *ethos* or to values of any kind. An artist's technique is test of his personal validity. Honesty of the word is the writer's first aim, for without it he can communicate nothing efficiently. His best velleity may be of no more avail than that of blurred men howling for peace, while abetting the murderers and mass starvers.

Orthology is a discipline both of *morale* and of morals.

2

Civilization begins when people start preferring a little done right to a great deal done wrong, as for example to Molinari's conducting, or that sort of thing in Salzburg to which brother Sheean objects. The aesthetic pleasure of hearing Bruno Walter play Mozart is about what one would derive from seeing a bust of Mozart carved in a sausage.

There is another pest, old music re-done for large orchestra: a miniature splodged out as a mural. At least we have had in our village, Rapallo, authentic presentations which gave one a basis for contemplating the composer. In parvo, what Toscanini does in the grand way. To hear Toscanini give Falstaff or Fidelio is part however of education. To hear any other man conduct these operas would probably be intolerable. They are both highly unsatisfactory to anyone with aural discretion of an high order. They are both, if authentically presented, essential parts of the education of anyone who wants to understand the history of OPERA as a form. The beastly Beethoven contributed to the development of the opera.

Let us by all means know it. Let us have the perfect rendering which leaves Ludwig no possible alibi. It is NOT a pleasant way of passing an evening but it is immeasurably instructive. It shows what poor Ludwig suffered.

Ditto Falstaff? No. NOT ditto. Falstaff is vindication of all Verdi's objections to Wagner. It is vindication of all Verdi's drive toward making a unity out of that heteroclite chaos of stage, orchestra, and caterwauling. Everything in it fits and belongs. It needs Toscanini, BUT it is second rate music. Not third rate. Given these two axes of reference one can be all the more justly severe on the inexcusable defects of nineteenth-century opera.

For the tenth time of saying it, the nauseous idiocy of composers is beyond anything a man can imagine until he himself has had a try at composing. The grossness of mind, the unending missing of continual opportunities is enough to produce black misanthropy.

Turning to Dr Whittaker's edition of William Young and his prefaces, we revive. Botticelli's 'Zephyrus' placates our parched audition. Young wrote for performers who were not virtuosi, but musicians capable of reading (that is of understanding) the musical line set before them.

Whittaker has blown the tags off the 'history' of the sonata. Dry datum, that, for the philologist. But he has also educed music for the auditor of discretion. Young says something in every few bars.

At the risk of thumping the pulpit, I reassert this distinction between art made for USE—that is painting to have painted into the plaster and stay while one lives there—and painting to stick in an exhibition to catch the eye of the passing possible buyer or vendor; music for who can play it and distinct from music made for the least common, and most vulgar, denominator of the herd in the largest possible hall. Having heard the original Janequin sung badly, I am inclined to wonder whether any chorus was ever sufficiently perfect in execution to give the intervals with the clarity of the fiddle, or if F. da Milano's lute could have rendered them as effectively. There is no valid reason for idolatry or antiquolatry. There is no reason why the re-creation of beauty should fall always below the original. The supposition that it does is half the time but fruit of a complex of inferiority in the sterile.

NOTE ON DANTE[1]

The *Divina Commedia* cannot comfortably be considered as an epic; to compare it with epic poems is usually unprofitable. It is in a sense lyric, the tremendous lyric of the subjective Dante; but the soundest classification of the poem is Dante's own, 'as a comedy which differs from tragedy in its content' (Epistle to Can Grande), for 'tragedy begins admirably and tranquilly', and the end is terrible, 'whereas comedy introduces some harsh complication, but brings the matter to a prosperous end'. The *Commedia* is, in a sense, a Mystery Play, or better, a cycle of mystery plays.

In the passages quoted I have tried to illustrate some, not all, of the qualities of its beauty, but Dante in English is Marsyas unsheathed.

Any sincere criticism of the highest poetry must resolve itself into a sort of profession of faith. The critic must begin with a *credo*, and his opinion will be received in part for the intelligence he may seem to possess, and in part for his earnestness. Certain of Dante's supremacies are comprehensible only to such as know Italian and have themselves attained a certain proficiency in the poetic art. An *ipse dixit* is not necessarily valueless. The penalty for remaining a layman is that one must at times accept a specialist's opinion. No one ever took

[1] From the end of a chapter "The Spirit of Romance", first published 1910.

196

the trouble to become a specialist for the bare pleasure of ramming his *ipse dixit* down the general throat.

There are two kinds of beautiful painting, as one may perhaps illustrate by the works of Burne-Jones and Whistler; one looks at the first kind of painting and is immediately delighted by its beauty; the second kind of painting, when first seen, puzzles one, but on leaving it, and going from the gallery one finds new beauty in natural things—a Thames fog, to use the hackneyed example. Thus, there are works of art which are beautiful objects, and works of art which are keys or passwords admitting one to a deeper knowledge, to a finer perception of beauty; Dante's work is of the second sort.

Presumably, critical analysis must proceed in part by comparison; Wordsworth is, we may say, the orthodox sign for comprehension of nature, yet where has Wordsworth written lines more instinct with 'nature-feeling' than those in the twenty-eighth of the *Purgatorio*.

> 'l' acqua diss' io, e il suon della foresta
> impugnan dentro a me novella fede.'

'The water, quoth I, and the woodland murmuring drive in new faith upon my soul.'

So one is tempted to translate it for the sake of the rhythm, but Dante has escaped the metaphysical term, and describes the actual sensation with more intensity. His words are:

> 'in-drive new faith within to me'.

Wordsworth and the Uncouth American share the palm for modern 'pantheism', or some such thing; but weigh their words with the opening lines of the *Paradiso*:

'La gloria di colui che tutto move
Per l' universo penetra e risplende
In una parte piu, e meno altrove.'

'The glory of him who moveth all
Penetrates and is resplendent through the all
In one part more and in another less.'

The disciples of Whitman cry out concerning the 'Cosmic sense', but Whitman, with all his catalogues and flounderings, has never so perfectly expressed the perception of cosmic consciousness as does Dante in the canto just quoted (i. 68–69):

'Qual si fe' Glauco nel gustar dell' erba
Che il fe' consorto in mar degli altri dei.'

'As Glaucus, tasting of the grass which made him sea-fellow of the other gods.'

Take it as simple prose expression, forget that it is told with matchless sound, discount the suggestion of the parallel beauty in the older myth, and it is still more convincing than Whitman.

Shelley, I believe, ranks highest as the English 'transcendental' poet, whatever that may mean. Shelley is honest in his endeavour to translate a part of Dante's meaning into the more northern tongue. He is, in sort, a faint echo of the *Paradiso*, very much as Rossetti is, at his best, an echo of the shorter Tuscan poetry. I doubt if Shelley ever thought of concealing the source of much of this beauty, which he made his own by appreciation. Certainly few men have honoured Dante more than did Shelley. 'The Ode to the West Wind' bears witness to his impressions of the earlier canti; thus to *Inferno* iii, of the host under the whirling ensign:

'Come d' autunno si levan le foglie
L' uno appreso dell' altra infin che il ramo
Vede alla terra tutte le sue spoglie.'

'As leaves of autumn fall one after one
Till the branch seeth all its spoils upon
The ground....'

The full passage from which this is taken foreshadows
the 'pestilence-stricken multitudes'.

'Ombre portate della detta briga,'

'Shadows borne upon the aforesaid strife,'

and the rest, with the movement of the wind, is pregnant
with suggestions for the English ode. This detracts
nothing from Shelley's glory, for of the tens of thousands
who have read these canti, only one has written such an
ode. This is not an isolated or a chance incident, the best
of Shelley is filled with memories of Dante.

The comparison of Dante and Milton is at best a stupid
convention. Shelley resembles Dante afar off, and in a
certain effect of clear light which both produce. Milton
resembles Dante in nothing; judging superficially, one
might say that they both wrote long poems which
mention God and the angels, but their gods and their
angels are as different as their styles and abilities. Dante's
god is ineffable divinity. Milton's god is a fussy old man
with a hobby. Dante is metaphysical, where Milton is
merely sectarian. *Paradise Lost* is conventional melo-
drama, and later critics have decided that the devil is
intended for the hero, which interpretation leaves the
whole without significance. Dante's satan is undeniably
and indelibly evil. He is not 'Free Will' but stupid

malignity. Milton has no grasp of the super-human. Milton's angels are men of enlarged power, plus wings. Dante's angels surpass human nature, and differ from it. They move in their high courses inexplicable.

> 'ma fe sembiante
> d' uomo, cui altra cura stringa'.

'Appeared as a man whom other care incites'.

(Inferno, ix. 101.)

Milton, moreover, shows a complete ignorance of the things of the spirit. Any attempt to compare the two poets as equals is bathos, and it is, incidentally, unfair to Milton, because it makes one forget all his laudable qualities.

Shakespeare alone of the English poets endures sustained comparison with the Florentine. Here we are with the masters; of neither can we say, 'He is the greater'; of each we must say, 'He is unexcelled.'

It is idle to ask what Dante would have made of writing stage plays, or what Shakespeare would have done with a 'Paradise'.

There is almost an exact three centuries between their dates of birth. (Dante, b. 1265; Shakespeare, 1564.) America had been discovered. The new forces: printing, the Reformation, the Renaissance were at work. Much change had swept over the world; but art and humanity, remaining largely the same, give us basis for comparison.

Dante would seem to have the greater imaginative 'vision', the greater ability to see the marvellous scenery through which his action passes; but Shakespeare's vision is never deficient, though his expression of it be confined to a few lines of suggestion and the prose of the stage directions.

Shakespeare would seem to have greater power in depicting various humanity, and to be more observant of its foibles; but recalling Dante's comparisons to the gamester leaving the play, to the peasant at the time of hoar-frost, to the folk passing in the shadow of evening, one wonders if he would have been less apt at fitting them with speeches. His dialogue is comparatively symbolic, it serves a purpose similar to that of the speeches in Plato, yet both he and Plato convey the impression of individuals speaking.

If the language of Shakespeare is more beautifully suggestive, that of Dante is more beautifully definite; both men are masters of the whole art. Shakespeare is perhaps more brilliant in his use of epithets of proper quality; thus I doubt if there be in Dante, or in all literature, any epithet so masterfully-placed as is Shakespeare's in the speech of the Queen Mother to Hamlet, where she says:

'And with the incorporal air do hold discourse,'

suggesting both the common void of the air which she sees and the ghostly form at which Hamlet stands aghast; on the other hand, Dante is, perhaps, more apt in 'comparison'.

'The apt use of metaphor, arising, as it does, from a swift perception of relations, is the hall-mark of genius.' I use the term 'comparison' to include metaphor, simile (which is a more leisurely expression of a kindred variety of thought), and the 'language beyond metaphor', that is, the more compressed or elliptical expression of metaphorical perception, such as antithesis suggested or implied in verbs and adjectives; for we find adjectives of two sorts, thus, adjectives of pure quality, as: white, cold, ancient; and adjectives which are comparative, as: lordly. Epithets may also be distinguished as epithets of primary and secondary apparition. By epithets of primary apparition I mean those which describe what is actually presented to the sense or vision. Thus in *selva oscura*, 'shadowy wood'; epithets of secondary apparition or after-thought are such as in '*sage* Hippotades' or '*forbidden* tree'. Epithets of primary apparition give vividness to description and stimulate conviction in the actual vision of the poet. There are likewise clauses and phrases of 'primary apparition'. Thus, in *Inferno* x, where Cavalcante di Cavalcanti's head appears above the edge of the tomb,

'credo che s' era in ginocchie levata',

'I believe he had risen on his knees',

has no beauty in itself, but adds greatly to the veri-similitude.

There are also epithets of 'emotional apparition', transensuous, suggestive: thus in Mr Yeats's line:

'Under a bitter *black* wind that blows from the left hand',

Dante's colouring and the qualities of the infernal air, although they are definitely symbolical and not in-definitely suggestive, foreshadow this sort of epithet. The modern symbolism is more vague, it is sometimes allegory in three dimensions instead of two, sometimes merely atmospheric suggestion.

It is in the swift forms of comparison, however, that Dante sets much of his beauty. Thus:

> 'dove il sol tace',
>
> 'where the sun is silent',

or,

> 'l' aura morta'.
>
> 'the dead air'.

In this last the comparison fades imperceptibly into emotional suggestion.

His vividness depends much on his comparison by simile to particular phenomena; this we have already noted in the chapter on Arnaut Daniel. Dante, following the Provençal, says, not 'where a river pools itself', but

> 'Si come ad Arli, ove il Rodano stagna.'
>
> 'As at Arles, where the Rhone pools itself.'

Or when he is describing not a scene but a feeling, he makes such comparison as in the matchless simile to Glaucus, already quoted.

Dante's temperament is austere, patrician; Shakespeare, as nature, combines refinement with profusion; it is as natural to compare Dante to a cathedral as it is to compare Shakespeare to a forest; yet Shakespeare is not more enamoured of out-of-door beauty than is Dante. Their lands make them familiar with a different sort of out-of-doors. Shakespeare shows his affection for this beauty as he knows it in—

> '—the morn, in russet mantle clad,
>
> Walks o'er the dew of yon high eastward hill';

and Dante, when the hoar frost

'paints her white sister's image on the ground'.

It is part of Dante's aristocracy that he conceded nothing to the world, or to opinion—

'si come avesse l' inferno in gran dispetto'

('as if he held hell in great disdain');

he met his reverses; Shakespeare concedes, succeeds, and repents in one swift, bitter line:

'I have made myself a motley to the view.'

Shakespeare comes nearer to most men, partly from his habit of speaking from inside his characters instead of conversing with them. He seems more human, but only when we forget the intimate confession of the *Vita Nuova* or such lines of the *Commedia* as

'col quale il fantolin corre alla mamma
quand' ha paura o quando egli è aflitto'.

'as the little child runs to its mother when it has fear, or when it is hurt'.

Dante has the advantage in points of pure sound; his onomatopœia is not a mere trick of imitating natural noises, but is a mastery in fitting the inarticulate sound of a passage to the mood or to the quality of voice which expresses that mood or passion which the passage expresses. Shakespeare has a language less apt for this work in pure sound, but he understands the motion of words, or, if the term be permitted, the overtones and undertones of rhythm, and he uses them with a mastery which no writer of English save Burns has come reasonably near to approaching. Other English poets master this part of the art occasionally, or as if by accident; as for example in the passage of Sturge Moore's 'Defeat of the Amazons', where the spirit of his faun leaps and scurries, with the words beginning:

'Ahi! ahi! ahi! Laomedon.'

This government of speed is a very different thing from the surge and sway of the epic music where the smoother rhythm is so merged with the sound quality as to be almost inextricable. The two things compare almost as the rhythm of a drum compares to the rhythm (not the sound) of the violin or organ. Thus, the 'surge and sway' are wonderful in Swinburne's first chorus in the *Atalanta*; while the other quality of word motion is most easily distinguished in, though by no means confined to, such poems as Burns' 'Birks o' Aberfeldy', where the actual sound-quality of the words contributes little or nothing to an effect dependent on the arrangement of quantities (i.e. the durations of syllables) and accent. It is not, as it might first seem, a question of vowel music as opposed to consonant music.

For those interested in 'sources', it may be well to write, once for all, that there is nothing particularly new in describing the journey of a living man through hell, or even of his translation into Paradise; Arda Virap, in the Zoroastrian legend, was sent as ambassador, in the most accredited fashion, with full credentials he ascended into Paradise, and saw the pains of hell shortly afterwards. The description of such journeys may be regarded as a confirmed literary habit of the race.

The question of Shakespeare's debt to Dante and the Tuscan poets is not of vital importance. It is true that a line of Shakespeare is often a finer expression of a Dantescan thought than any mere translator of Dante has hit upon, but nothing is more natural than that the two greatest poets of Christendom, holding up their mirrors to nature, should occasionally reflect the same detail. It is true that Shakespeare's lines:

'What is your substance, whereof are you made,
That millions of strange shadows on you tend?'

seem like a marriage of words from Guido Orlando's sonnet to Guido Cavalcanti, and from one of Cavalcanti's sonnets which I have quoted. Mascetta Caracci has written a thesis on 'Shakespeare ed i classici Italiani', multiplying instances.

Early Tuscan sonnets are often very 'Elizabethan', and the Spanish imitations of the Tuscans are often more so. Great poets seldom make bricks without straw; they pile up all the excellences they can beg, borrow, or steal from their predecessors and contemporaries, and then set their own inimitable light atop of the mountain. It is possible that the author of *The Sonnets* was ignorant of the finest sonnets in the world, and that Shakespeare may have read Bandello and not the Italian masters. Shakespeare knew of Gower, and Gower and Chaucer knew of Dante. As Shakespeare wrote the finest poetry in English, it matters not one jot whether or no he plundered the early rather than the later Italian lyrists in his general sack of the literature then available in London.

That Shakespeare, as Dante, is the conscious master of his art is most patent from the manner in which he plays with his art in the sonnets, teasing, experimenting, developing that technique which he so marvellously uses and so cunningly conceals in the later plays. To talk about 'wood-notes wild' is sheer imbecility.

Did Shakespeare know his Tuscan poetry directly or through some medium, through Petrarch, or through some Italianized Englishman? Why did he not write a play on Francesca da Rimini? There are a number of subjects for amusing speculation; theories will be built from straws floating in the wind; thus Francis Meres, when in 1598 he writes of Shakespeare's 'fine-filed phrase', may or may not have some half memory of Dante's *amorosa lima*, the 'loving file' that had 'polished his speech'.

Our knowledge of Dante and of Shakespeare interacts; intimate acquaintance with either breeds that discrimination which makes us more keenly appreciate the other.

One might indefinitely continue the praise of Dante's excellence of technique and his splendours of detail; but beneath these individual and separate delights is the great sub-surge of his truth and his sincerity: his work is of that sort of art which is a key to the understanding of nature, of the beauty of the world and of the spirit. From his descriptions of the aspects of nature I have already quoted the passage of the sunlight and the cloud shadows.